BEAT

How to hear the music
of your heart

Bernadette Somers

To my two loves,
May the beat of your hearts
Live on in these words.

First published in 2022 by Bernadette Somers

bernadettesomers.com

© Bernadette Somers 2022

The moral rights of the author have been asserted

All rights reserved. Except as permitted under the *Australian Copyright Act 1968* (for example, a fair dealing for the purposes of study, research, criticism or review), no part of this book may be reproduced, stored in a retrieval system, communicated or transmitted in any form or by any means without prior written permission.

All inquiries should be made to the author.

A catalogue entry for this book is available from the National Library of Australia.

 A catalogue record for this book is available from the National Library of Australia

ISBN: 978-0-6456703-1-8

Published in Australia by Mono Unlimited (www.monounlimited.com)

Cover artwork by Chloe Planinsek

The paper this book is printed on is certified as environmentally friendly.

Disclaimer: The material in this publication is of the nature of general comment only, and does not represent professional advice. It is not intended to provide specific guidance for particular circumstances and it should not be relied on as the basis for any decision to take action or not take action on any matter which it covers. Readers should obtain professional advice where appropriate, before making any such decision. To the maximum extent permitted by law, the author and publisher disclaim all responsibility and liability to any person, arising directly or indirectly from any person taking or not taking action based on the information in this publication.

'Music can change the world.'

LUDWIG VAN BEETHOVEN

Resources

MY SONGS

1. Beat
2. I See You
3. Petals
4. Still with Me
5. Go to Sleep
6. Mother Mary
7. Matter
8. Lonely Life
9. Parts
10. Differentt
11. Underwater

Download all the original songs in this book from
www.bernadettesomers.com/resources
or scan this QR code:

QR codes to download individual songs
on Spotify are also included inside the book.

BEAT

Can you hear the music of your heart
Playing to an everlasting beat
Can you hear the music of all hearts
Running through your head and to your feet

Can you hear all hearts that beat as one
Can you feel the beat upon the street
Can you feel the force that draws us home
The feeling that connects us to the beat

Hear Mother Mary sing, she sings a song for you
Hear the angels sing, they sing a song for you

Beat
Beat
Beat
Beat

Can you let the music take you higher
Can you feel connected to the light
Hear the angels singing in the choir
Feel the beat, feel the delight

Hear Mother Mary sing, she sings a song for you
Hear the angels sing, they sing a song for you
Hear Mother Mary sing, she sings a song for you
Hear the angels sing, they sing a song for you

Beat
Beat
Beat
It's the beat

Join the beat
It's the beat
We are the beat
We are the beat

BERNADETTE SOMERS

DOWNLOAD
'BEAT'
ON SPOTIFY

Contents

Preface 1

Definitions 7

    Let it Be 8

    Danny Boy 13

    Isn't She Lovely 17

    I Need You To Turn To 20

    You're the Voice 22

    I'm Kissing You 26

    Prepare Ye the Way of the Lord 30

    Amazing Grace 34

    All You Need is Love 39

    The Rose 43

    Cry Me a River 47

    One Day at a Time 51

The Power 59

A Sky Full of Stars 64

Heavy on My Heart 69

Healing Hands 74

Staying Alive 77

I Got You Babe 80

Candle in the Wind 83

Never Tear Us Apart 90

Like a Virgin 96

Beautiful 100

Miss Celie's Blues 107

Bridge over Troubled Water 111

Bohemian Rhapsody 115

Read All About It 121

My Way 124

The Way We Were 127

Sing 131

Here Comes the Sun 134

Nothing Breaks Like a Heart 139

Tiny Dancer 143

CONTENTS

The Twelfth of Never 145

Fly Like an Eagle 147

Money Money Money 151

Perfect 155

Under Pressure 158

Stairway to Heaven 161

Heal Me 163

Even Flow 167

Fix You 170

Brave 176

Heart of Stone 180

Unchained Melody 184

A Final Word 188

Acknowledgements 191

About the Author 192

Preface

This book has a gentle unfolding.
    Of my songs, to you.
    Of my heart, to you.
    In the stories.
    In the songs.

    If you read on and allow my heart to open for you, as I share my songs, your heart might open too, and that might move you closer to the beat. If we all open our hearts and hear the universe beat for us, we might find our way home.
    Finding a way home feels very much like returning back to the warmth of the mother's womb, right near the beat.
    Where all is safe.
    All is well.
    Near the beat.

    Beat.
    This book is for those who long to surrender to the innate rhythm and beat within.
    The beat of the heart.
    The beat of the music.
    The beat on the street.
    The beat to which we all synchronise in order to allow life flow,

like blood through our veins.

This book is as much about the heart as it is about the music. It is about my songs that become your songs. It is about the music that speaks to us all in a language our hearts understand.

This book is for all who hear the beat, feel the beat, and dream of songs and lyrics. It is for those who are unshakeably and irreversibly moved by music, its sound, its frequency, its vibration, its parts, its symphony.

For those who can't fully describe how much music lifts them up and takes them to places where they long to stay.

For those who feel connected to others through the shared joy and beat of music.

For those who relate a song to a time, a place, or an evolutionary stage in their lives.

For those who want to revel in the memories that the music evokes.

For those who long to travel back to places and spaces where the beat transported them.

And finally…

For those who are ready to connect with the beat of their hearts and find their way home…

to the beat

through the beat

with the beat

in the beat

as the beat.

There is music playing for us all. There are notes arising from every voice. There are hearts ready to open.

All is waiting.

Who is ready for the beat?

Let's begin to sync back into the beat.

Never is there a time like now.

PREFACE

A time to find more meaning from the beat, to honour our own heart beats, to honour the sounds, to honour our own sounds in response to the music.

To let go.

To let out the sounds.

To open up and surrender all.

To forget our troubles and worries and get back in sync. To sync back into the innate beat and let it carry us in the sound waves, carry us to a place where we forget and then remember what's really important.

It is time.

And time is upon us.

I sat at the piano.
I let her speak.
She quietly and gently played through me.
I opened my mouth and the words came out.
I opened my heart and the beat came out.
And out flew the songs of generations.
Flying like birds beating their wings.

I followed the beat.
And it led me home.

BERNADETTE SOMERS

PREFACE

Ever since man first walked this earth, I believe he inherently knew about the beat. I have an image that sticks in my mind. It's of my ancestors and your ancestors retrieving stones from the ground. I see them bring the stones together and create a beat.

I hear this beat… primal, tribal, innate, calling.

I watch the beat bring the tribe together, all feeling the calling of the sound, reminding them of the beat of their mothers' hearts.

I believe this beat, the sound, is the collective force that brings a tribe together.

I believe it brings people together too. The beat underpins the union, assists in the unity.

I believe that our need to belong to a tribe is as innate as the beat of our own hearts.

I have another image I see. It is the tribe moving to the beat. I see the dance, the motion, the ceremony and the ritual. I feel the workings of the beat reach the beat of their hearts. And the movement cannot be stopped. It moves like blood pumping through all chambers. It is as innate as the beat.

When musicians are learning to play an instrument, they have to learn to 'hold the beat' in order to bring it to life. They have to hear the beat, connect to it, reverberate with it, integrate with it and lose themselves in it. It is a mystical thing when they unite with other musicians to collectively hold the beat, just as our ancestors did, holding the tribal beat together. Moving to it, dancing to it, syncing to it.

Everything in life has its own unique vibration and vibrations have their own frequency—this is sound. Our ancestors knew this, learnt this and passed it through the generations. It is in our history, our blood, our beat, close to our hearts.

Sound heals us.

The beat connects us.

So, it is my wish. If we can hold the beat together and make

BEAT

music, we have the potential to hold together in many other ways.

If we can open our hearts to the beat, we have the potential to remain open to receive in many other ways.

This is my wish.

This is my beat.

This is the beat for all.

Definitions

Beat: a main accent or rhythmic unit in music.

: a pulsation of the heart

: to overcome

Let It Be *

We are all familiar with this beautiful song *Let It Be* by the Beatles. But are we familiar with how this song came to be?

Let It Be was written by Paul McCartney after he dreamt about his departed mother, Patricia. In the dream, Patricia said the words to him, 'It will be alright, just let it be.' Life gifted him the song whist he slept and he woke and penned the words to the melody.

The origin of this beautiful song is from somewhere that is hard to fathom. It's the place or space in the universe that delivers inspirations to recipients. Perhaps they have asked for the inspiration, perhaps they are chosen. Perhaps they were always destined to be the recipient, or perhaps they ushered in the gift.

Perhaps it's the process whereby life gifts someone who has their arms stretched wide open to ask and their heart stretched wide open to receive.

Perhaps we may never quite fully understand and that remains the magic or mysticism of it all.

When I find myself in times of trouble, I hear a voice saying words to me. It isn't the voice of Patricia McCartney, or the voice

---

* Written by John Lennon and Paul McCartney, 1970. Publisher: Sony/ATV Music Publishing LLC Paul McCartney and John Lennon Quoted under Fair Use Act.

of Mother Mary, but it sounds like the voice of a divine mother or maternal source that assures me all is well. I like to call it life talking, whispering, in fact, as I need to be quiet and still to really hear it.

I think that is the point, to be quiet and still, in order to really hear. When I really tune in, it brings me peace. Perhaps it's like being back in the womb, quiet, safe, still— not speaking but really listening, and always hearing the safety and the continuance of the mother's heartbeat in the background, filling the space with sound.

If there is one certainty in life, it is this. We were all born from the mother. Her heartbeat is the first sound we ever hear, and it is to this beat or rhythm that we grow. It is from that beat that we are nourished. That beat that is our life force. We sync to that beat. We learn to move in her body and stretch in her waters. We learn to move to the continual beat that provides the backdrop to life. We all relate to that feeling of being held by the mother.

Let It Be and Paul McCartney's lyrics take us to that place, that feeling, that beat. The words remind us of our deep, internal need to be held, to be nurtured, to be loved. They remind us of a deep desire to be both independent of the mother but to always be close to her heart. I think it's the feeling of being close to the beat. That is the point of this book, this song and of life itself.

Songs, words and lyrics can conjure up emotions that transport us back to our childhood memories of times when we needed and received maternal love and care. Songs have such magical power and the lyrics can help heal us.

If there were some words of loving guidance needed to be heard from the mother, they would be… 'there will always be an answer, just let it be'.

I hope that my words can usher back in those words, for you. I hope that this song can fly on in on the wings of the birds and open your heart to hear the music.

I hope that it sits close to your heartbeat and brings you the feeling of maternal love.

Love is a feeling and music can make you feel it.

All you need is the beat.

I have loved music since I was a little girl.

My parents purchased a piano or 'pianola' when I was twelve years old, and I very quickly learnt to love the sound of the piano. I think it could have been a love for any musical instrument, it was more about me finding my love for creating music.

The pianola, of course, could play music by pushing the foot pedals and putting in a paper roll of music. It was that easy to make the piano keys dance. Most of the rolls of music available were from songs of the olden days, songs that would make many a dear grandmother tap her feet to the beat.

For me, the pianola was magical, and it paved the way for me to learn to play the piano by ear. It opened several doors and little did I know that songs would come through me to me: songs with little warning and no planning. This doorway would enable songs to be played for me, by me. All I had to do to allow this was to open my heart, to connect to my own heartbeat.

The process is very similar to how *Let It Be* arrived in a dream for Paul McCartney, through some sort of channel.

The way songs would arrive for me, with no formal musical training, felt mystical and somewhat unbelievable. But after many years of experiencing this magic, I now have my own understanding of the process.

You see, I believe that all songs and melodies are waiting in the wings, in the sphere, the void, portal or channel, ready to be delivered to those who are ready, willing and open to receive them.

Those who are 'able' to receive. The 'able' part of this equation has an expansive eligibility, as I am proof.

LET IT BE

If you are willing to open your heart and participate in receiving inspirations from the divine, your musical skills are not under scrutiny. It's all about having your heart open. This opens the doorway to receive the beat, to sync into the natural source of all things.

So, I like to believe the addition of the piano to my family home was divinely orchestrated and many of my teenage years were spent playing the keys of this instrument and finding my voice to sing.

It was the beginning of a deep, abiding love story that still continues to this day.

I progressed from pianola to keyboard to my own piano: the gift from my husband on my fortieth birthday.

Currently in a house full of four children, the only space for my piano to reside is in my own bedroom, which is fitting since my bedroom has become the absolute spiritual hub of my home. It is the place where I sit to write songs. It is the place I sat to write my first book, *Yolk* and it is where I have written *Beat*.

So, it is very fitting that I also channel or receive music in this place, on my piano.

That piano, in the corner of my bedroom, is the place for music to emerge. It flies on in and lands in my heart. And when I finally learnt to find my voice, I was able to bring all my parts to life.

This took many years, many challenges, and much growth and personal evolution. It took the birthing of my book *Yolk* to put words into form, and so it is the perfect progression to now put musical words into form—into *Beat*.

They say that music lights you up and we all have our own unique light language.

It took me many years to understand that music, singing and songs were a form of my light language.

When you share your light, you have tapped into the source of the things that fill you up. It is aligned with your purpose, and it is also aligned with the words a gentle mother—like the one in *Let It Be*—would encourage you to be.

It is like the way the gentle mother would remind you to let it be. Let yourself be you, whatever that is. Be authentically you. Be your authentic expression. Do what you love. Be in your own lane. In your flow. Aligned, aligning. Being you, always, in all ways.

The 'all ways' of the equation is your own light language. And mine is music. I am aligned to the beat, and it is why I felt guided to write this book. I know in my heart that there are many of you like me. You also feel the collective pull of music. You feel it deeply ingrained in you. You need music in your life. And it does more for you than you can put in words. And so, I am here to put it in words for us all, to transmute and encode the beat, to articulate the feeling. I am doing this for me so I can fully comprehend, but I am doing it for you too, so that it makes sense, so that it opens your door to receive more, so that we all connect to the beat.

I hope this book and the beat can do that for you.

Danny Boy [*]

The first keys that my small fingers ever touched were that of my grandparents' piano. It is of no irony that the address of my grandparents' home was 8 Nirvana Crescent, 8 being the number of luck and nirvana meaning heaven.

My love affair with the piano began here at 8 Nirvana Crescent in the back spare room of my grandparents Jim and Isobel's home.

I think many people forged their own love affair with the piano from their grandparents. The piano used to be the centrepiece of connection and entertainment, long before the television or the internet.

Sometimes when I am dreaming or in deep meditation, the recesses of my mind transport me back to this room with the piano. I become the observer looking in at the brown piano, its lid ajar, ready and waiting for its keys to be anointed. Waiting for the magic to start.

My nana Isobel was a kind, happy lady with a smile and laughter that could light up a room. She had this way of leaning her upper body on the kitchen bench as she laughed at the antics of her adult sons, one being my dad. She laughed at both small things and at herself, a quality that made her all the more endearing.

---

[*] Music: Londonderry Air., lyrics by Frederick Weatherly, 1913. Public domain. Quoted under Fair Use Act.

I always see her in wool, of a pale sky-blue colour, soft, warm and comforting. When my nan hugged me, I felt fully enveloped by her, by the plump folds of her skin, by her warm nurturing love. An embrace of the grandmother. Felt deep to the core. I have the most vivid memories of watching my nan play the piano in the back room at 8 Nirvana Crescent. Her bottom and thighs filled the small piano stool and her arms stretched out to reach the deepest and highest keys like a bird unfurling its wings.

I remember Nan playing *Danny Boy*. This song has become her song. It always conjures up memories of her in her blue woollen cardigan, happily twinkling the piano keys.

I think that *Danny Boy*, the beloved Irish ballad, has its roots embedded in my nan's Irish ancestry.

I believe the song stirs a feeling in the hearts of all the Irish, like the song connects all of their heartbeats. The words, "Come ye back" are actually prophetic because every time I listen to the song, the memories of my nan come flooding back.

I believe that our departed live on in the music, in their songs, which evoke memories of them. I almost feel enveloped in the fold of my Nana's embrace as I lose myself in the song.

I know my introduction to the piano and my observation of Nana playing are an integral part of my own story, my own legacy. The piano has become my own place of solace, my place to pour out my emotions, as if talking to a departed loved one or feeling their embrace.

The piano has become my vehicle to birth songs that come from some place outside of myself where they no longer wish to wait. It feels as if they need motion and movement, sound and light. I think I am the light, or at least this has been explained to me by many spiritual teachers. I think the inspiration is drawn to the light, then it releases. I know that an open heart lets in the light. I know this with certainty.

DANNY BOY

The rest of the workings of this process are mystical, but one thing I am sure of is this: my connection with the piano in the back room of 8 Nirvana Crescent was not by chance. It was interwoven in my story. And it becomes Nan's story. It brings her back with the song—her *Danny Boy*—and with her piano.

And she becomes part of the beat.

With the beat, we all have the opportunity to bring back our departed loved ones. Their hearts may no longer be beating, but the continuance of the beat in their songs is part of their continuance. The beat of the music continues, and so do they.

Rest in peace Nana.

Your music enveloped all your grandchildren in notes of love.

Place your hand on your heart.
Feel the beat.
Breathe it in.
Stay there for as long as you need.
Come back here whenever you need
The beat is yours.

BERNADETTE SOMERS

Isn't She Lovely [*]

Stevie Wonder wrote *Isn't She Lovely* to celebrate the birth of his daughter Aisha.

The name Aisha means 'life' or 'alive' and the beat of the heart is the sign of life.

His baby girl was less than one minute old and in that same moment, Stevie Wonder understood how lovely and precious a new life is.

I understood this, myself, in less than a minute, many years back.

It was a night in mid-1987 that I first witnessed a life enter the world: a baby girl, and this moment changed me forever.

For as long as I can remember I was fascinated by pregnancy and birth. I feel it was wired into my DNA from a very young age. It was also the catalyst for me to pursue a career in physiotherapy as a means to progress towards working in women's health and obstetrics.

I forged through four years of study until I finally got to partake in an elective of Obstetrics and Gynaecology at a hospital in Clayton, Victoria. Normally these clinical placements were allocated based on your proximity to the hospital's location. However, a fortuitous

---

[*] Written by Stevie Wonder, 1976. Publisher: Black Bull Music, O/B/O CAPASSO, Songtrust Ave, Sony/ATV Music Publishing LLC. Quoted under Fair Use Act.

and synchronistic moment lead to my placement being changed to the hospital in Clayton. During this placement I would find myself walking the corridors of the hospital with a deep, conclusive knowing that I would one day work as a physiotherapist at this hospital.

You might resonate with this feeling of not knowing how, not knowing when and not knowing why, but knowing.

I have had many 'no doubt in my mind' moments since then, but this one was one of my first. Little did I know at the time that at this very hospital I would connect with a friend who would go on to meet my brother and become his wife. I would connect with another person who I would form a business with. And lastly, I would meet the obstetrician who would go on to deliver all four of my children. It was all meant to be. And it was that obstetrician whom I watched tend to the pregnant, labouring mother-to-be in the delivery suite on that day in 1987.

I never forget the care and love this doctor showed this woman, and I will never forget the moment of witnessing a new life entering the world.

Isn't She Lovely begins with the sound of a newborn baby's cry, and that sound filled both the room and my heart, late into the night of that special day in 1987.

It solidified a few things for me: I would not leave this earth without being a mother and this obstetrician would be the man who assisted in bringing this dream to fruition.

You see, life begins as soon as there is a beat. It's the sound that all parents-to-be most want to hear at an ultrasound scan. It's the sound the soothes the anxious mum-to-be in the delivery suite, willing the baby to make safe passage into her arms.

As I drove home from the hospital, late into the night of that day in 1987, weary from the emotional high of witnessing a birth, I turned on my car radio and heard the song, *Isn't She Lovely* by Stevie Wonder.

ISN'T SHE LOVELY?

I realised that the event I had just witnessed was indeed made from love as the song implies; the love between this couple to bring this baby to life, the love shown by the doctor to usher her in, and the love shown by Stevie Wonder to pen a song about his new baby girl.

It made me understand that all things made with love are so incredibly precious.

And this newborn baby girl and the song both live through the beat.

A beat of a song.
A beat of a new heart.
Both made with love.

I Need You To Turn To [*]

In the song *I Need You To Turn To*, Elton John sings of a guardian angel that keeps out the cold. My husband, Mark, is exactly that for me.

The first time I ever visited the house that would become my home, this song was playing.

In hindsight, I now realise that I did need someone to turn to, and Mark, this beautiful man, who showed his deeper side by showing me his choice of song, became that person for me.

I remember first visiting Mark's home and taking it all in, including the sounds of the song he chose to play for me. I remember the way he decorated the rooms, the paintings, the trinkets, the soft couch, the warm bed and lastly, his CD collection. I believe you can read a lot about someone from seeing their music collection.

I love that he chose the music for us to listen to, as we sat together, learning more about the person that would end up being their other half. I did not know the song he played for me. I did not know that this song would lead me to him. I did not know that this song would be the one I would hear as I walked down the aisle to find Mark waiting to make me his wife.

I did not know that the home that was filled with his music would

---

[*] Written by Bernie Taupin and Elton John, 1970. © Universal Music Publishing Group. Quoted under Fair Use Act.

soon become my home too and we would raise our family here.

I could not have for seen all the magical memories that were being made in this place and space I was visiting for the first time.

But I did know one thing. The song landed. It managed to frame a moment in time and attach beautiful memories to it. It became the memory, and now when this song is played, the memory floods back in as if I am back there in the home I once lived in, back in the room where I sat and listened to the beat, with the man who would become the one I always turn to.

Songs have the power to transport us back to spaces across timelines.

You might have a song that delivers you to a time in your life where the feelings are delivered to you all over again. It might feel as if you are travelling across, over and beyond all your current challenges.

The remembering might help you to forget.

The forgetting might help you to remember.

You can choose to feel the joy, happiness and love all over again. You just have to play your song; you just have to sync back to the beat. And when you do, it opens your heart. And through that open heart, it is not only the music that arrives, but so much more, as this book will illustrate.

If you can be transported by a beat of a song, imagine what else the beat can do.

I will always need music in my life, as I need the beat to turn to, just like I need the memory of this song to transport me back.

If you feel like I do, play your song.

Join in the beat. See where it takes you.

You're the Voice *

I love stories of synchronicity. They make my heart kind of flutter. They give me this deep sense of peace knowing that some kind of higher power has a hand in how things are playing out, that it's not all just in my own hands.

The story of synchronicity occurred at a time in my life when fear and doubt tried to interfere, and I really needed to feel the full force of those 'hands' pushing me in the direction I needed to go.

It was July 2018, and I was lucky enough to attend a Hay House writers' workshop course held in Melbourne, my own hometown. My affinity with the words of Louise Hay and the opportunity to attend a course in Melbourne meant that I knew I was supposed to be at this workshop. I had a half-written book and a small pipedream to publish it, but other than that, had no clear idea on how I was going to make it all happen.

A few years prior I had gone to see a psychic medium who lived nearby. During her session she had mentioned that she saw books around me and asked me if I had considered writing a book. I could honestly say that at that time in my life I had never ever considered writing a book and did not feel her words planted any seed that

---

* Written by Andy Qunta, Chris Thompson, Keith Reid and Maggie Ryder, 1986. Publisher: Bucks Music Group, Royalty Network. Quoted under Fair Use Act.

made me consider it. But she did encourage me to begin the process of writing in a journal, so that I could get some clarity with my thoughts.

So, the next day, I bought a journal, and began writing. From that daily practice of writing every day, my book began to take form. It was so unplanned and unannounced, it seemed as if the process of writing had unlocked something in me that gave birth to 'the writer'.

I think it was exactly like the process that happened for Paul McCartney with *Let It Be*. It was as if life began to speak, and I began to dictate what it said. I became life's secretary in a way, transcribing its words and making them my own. But I really take no credit for the words, they come through me as they come to me. They don't start as mine but they become mine. They need a secretary, and I am very happy to be one.

So, as synchronicity would have it, in the one spare seat in the auditorium next to me was the same psychic medium who had delivered the guidance about writing in a journal. We spent the weekend together at the workshop and reconnected. I could not have known that I would also become a medium and work in a very similar way to the way that she worked.

My secretarial role would take on a new slant, receiving messages from the departed. But first, I had to birth the book.

The guest speaker at the workshop was an author, Rebecca Campbell, a beautiful woman proudly out of her spiritual closet, unapologetically owning every word in her wonderful books. I had much inner work to do to get to this level and knew that publishing my own spiritual book was going to expediate this growth process for me.

Rebecca spoke of a song she wished to play to the attendees that would become the theme song for all the writers in the room. She invited people up onto the stage join her and sing the song.

She played *You're the Voice* by John Farnham, a song that I love, and everyone sang the words.

I knew that the words of the song were a message for me. I felt it course through my blood. It was time not to live in silence or in fear of finding my voice. I felt as if Rebecca was looking straight at me, willing me to come out of my spiritual closet and join her in the beat.

I have only ever felt certain about anything in my life a handful of times, and this was one of those times.

I had to write my book.

I went home after the workshop and finished writing my book *Yolk*. and a few weeks later I was ready to get a copy printed.

I am very aware of numbers. They are 'my thing'.

I see 4 and all its iterations all the time, especially 44. I am the fourth child in my family, and I have 4 children. I am born on the 16th, which is a multiple of 4 (4x4). I am named after Saint Bernadette, and her feast day is on the 16th of April, the fourth month. Whenever I need validation, I see 4 and mainly 44. And my all-time favourite, synchronistic number to see is 11:44.

Some of you will relate and have your own numbers. They are just another way for life to get your attention.

So, on the day I went to get my manuscript printed, I was feeling very emotional. I felt a deep sense of accomplishment that I had finished something that required a lot of courage to complete. It wasn't the writing so much, it was more the reveal of my true self in the writing.

It felt like coming out from that spiritual closet. It felt deeply revealing and vulnerable to share. It felt like I was sharing my own sacred understanding of how life whispered to me, and this in itself was a significant step.

I think we have various-sized steps as we walk our path. Some feel easy and 'step-able', others feel like giant leaps. We probably get the most growth from the big steps, but they are often the hardest to complete. This was a giant, 'I need a big kind of preparatory run up', leap for me. And I was feeling all of these emotions as I sat in the car with my printed manuscript on my lap.

As my husband started the ignition of the car to drive me home, my phone screen lit up with the time of 11:44 am, as the song *You're the Voice* played on the radio of my husband's car.

I wept.

The synchronicity made me weep tears of joy, pain and realisation that not everything was held in my hands. I knew right then that life held me and so much of this synchronicity in its hands for me. I knew I was on my path and this step was one step closer to taking me in the direction life was ushering me.

As an attendee of the writers' workshop, I was given the opportunity to enter a submission of my book in order to win a publishing deal. The cut-off date for the submission was my husband's birthday, 10 December. It felt like another synchronicity that reminded me that I was on track.

As fate would have it, I celebrated my husband's birthday listening to John Farnham perform at *A Day on the Green*, a music festival hosted at the Yarra Valley. When John sang *You're the Voice*, I felt the most amazing sense of peace and happiness.

I had done the work.

I had found my voice.

I had written my book.

I sang my heart out that day and connected to the beat. I sang for my younger self that would never have had the courage to sing or write.

I now listen to that song and I sing the words to myself.

It is my anthem.

I am going to spend my days writing and singing and doing the things that I love. I am going to share what I write and what I sing. And it doesn't matter about my voice, it matters that life finds its voice through me.

I'm Kissing You *

I have always loved anything and everything to do with pregnancy and childbirth. Maybe it was something to do with being born into a family of seven children, witnessing my mother's three pregnancies after me. I am not entirely sure, but I have always loved babies and the whole process of how they come to be.

My life has been driven by the deep desire to be a mother and to be involved somehow in the process of other women trying to become mothers. I always wanted to be a midwife but chose to become a women's health physiotherapist instead. This enabled me to follow women through all life cycles, not only the childbirth cycle. I loved teaching childbirth education classes and preparing women for labour and birth. I always encouraged them to prepare a music playlist to have in the delivery suite. It seemed fitting to have a beat accompanying the impending beat of the newborn baby's heart. I believed that music played an important role in keeping the mother calm and centred during the labour.

I fell pregnant very quickly after marrying my husband Mark, and our firstborn son, Joshua was born one month after our first wedding anniversary.

In preparation for my own labour, I put together a playlist of

---

* Written by Des'ree and Timothy Atack, 1996. Publisher: Fox Music, Inc, Kobalt Music Publishing Ltd. Quoted under Fair Use Act.

all my favourite songs to listen to during the delivery. Back then the music was played on a cassette tape on a big beat box player. I carefully chose all songs that evoked some emotional response from me, as music does and always will do. Music has always connected me to myself and something bigger.

At 38 week's gestation my husband and I decided to go to the cinema and watch *Romeo and Juliet*, starring Leonardo Di Caprio. I was a bit uncomfortable seated in the cinema chair as my son was pressing down on my pelvic bones and taking up all of my internal space. But when a beautiful song began to play on the screen, I completely forgot about my discomfort and proceeded to lose myself in the melody. I was completely transfixed by this song, and I shed tears listening to the tune, which was not difficult to do given the pregnancy hormones coursing through my blood stream.

As the song finished, I felt the most intense pain deep in my pelvis. It felt as if the effect of the song had created such a visceral response in my body that it had activated something in my unborn son. He began to move into position for delivery. I did not know at the time that this would be a courageous and difficult move for him, as his head and body were in a posterior position, so that meant his turning circle only allowed him to wedge himself in slightly sideways.

I sat in the cinema in agony for another half an hour until he finally became still. When we returned home from the movie, I was intent on discovering the name of the song I had heard. It was *I'm Kissing You* by Des'ree, and I immediately added it to my playlist for the birth.

Two weeks later I was in the delivery suite listening to that song after hours and hours of poorly progressing labour. I was at my tipping point, trying to breathe, trying to use the tools and practices I taught women to use in the classes. But my baby was stuck in the wrong position, wedged inside my pelvis, and was going to require a forceps delivery.

When the song began to play in that delivery suite, at that moment of pain and frustration, I lost the plot. I cried, I howled, and I got lost in the collective misery and agony of every woman who had laboured and suffered in order to bring life into this world.

I sobbed for the entire length of the song. It activated something in me, just as it had activated something in my unborn child when I first heard the tune. It made me understand that the beginning and the end of life, no matter who you are, involves some degree of suffering. Suffering of the mother as life is given. Suffering of the person as life is taken. I sobbed tears for the collective, during *I'm Kissing You*. I also realised that it's the one small act of love we all wish to show at both times: kissing our newborns, kissing our dying loved ones.

This will always remain a song that reminds me of the birth of my beautiful firstborn son, Joshua. It will always be the song that reminds me of the full gamut of human emotion, the pain, the tears, the grief, the joy, and the exquisite love found on both sides of life arriving and life leaving.

That is the power of a song. That is the power of music. That is the power of the beat.

> A heart's first beat in a moment
> A heart's last beat in a moment

Life is as fleeting as a song playing, as fleeting as a moment. Enjoy every beat.

Whenever I lose myself in the music
A part of me finds its way home.

BERNADETTE SOMERS

Prepare Ye the Way of the Lord *

I always loved to sing, even as a child. I remember when I was young, the musical *Godspell* was released, and I was captivated by its songs and the lyrics.

I loved to sing with my cousins at family gatherings and we would pretend to do performances of the songs from *Godspell* whilst playing in my bedroom.

I shared a long dormitory-shaped bedroom with my two older sisters in which our wardrobes and desks would provide a subdivision to the space. My father was a builder and had designed this clever L-shaped upstairs space that allocated an individual room space for his three sons and three daughters. This worked beautifully for the family of six children until the seventh child was conceived and the design required some redeliberation.

The long room had three short curtains lining the windows out to the back garden. My cousins and I could use these curtains as our stage curtains. We loved to pull the curtain cord and present ourselves for our performance of *Prepare Ye the Way of the Lord*. We sang in sequence and with great gusto. We sang about preparing

---

* Written by Stephen Schwartz and John Michael Tebelak, 1971. Published by Quartet Music, Range Road Music Inc, S & J Legacy Productions LLC. Quoted under Fair Use Act.

a way to the Lord. It was not that we were overly religious, we just enjoyed singing the words to the song and we liked to have our performance perfectly timed. We were preparing and finding our voices in the upstairs bedroom of my family home. We were preparing to perform the song to our parents and use our voices.

I often think back to this time and this performance. I think back to that young girl, preparing and singing with such confidence and joy. I now see the parallels; I was finding my voice. I think all of my younger years were preparing to sing the songs to the beat, to find my voice, to prepare the way.

My understanding of it is that I was not so much preparing 'the way of the Lord', but I was preparing my own understanding of God, as a feeling, in my heart, close to the beat. I was preparing to learn one way to God through religion, to then lose that, and then find another way.

I was preparing to learn that it was not about God, the man, but entirely about God as the feeling, of love. I was preparing to navigate a way forward to move closer to my own understanding of it all. While my understanding is my own and may not be for you, I am sharing it here with you in case it helps you with your own understanding.

Preparing a way to the Lord feels like preparing a pathway through my heart which warms me and brings me close, right next to the beat. It's deep within me. It's where the love is found. It feels as if I have been preparing my whole life to find this place in my heart and find this truth. I have been preparing to find the love. Not through religion, but through my heart. It feels as if this is my only way and that the words in this book are meant to crystalise this for me.

I feel prepared, and so now, I sing. It's fitting that this chapter 'prepares' both myself and you for my song share in the next chapter.

BEAT

I have prepared the way, and I think we are all somehow initiated or prepared for the beat. It's innate, and it's ready for us to sync to it.

So, my hope is that the beat also prepares you to find your own understanding of your beat and your heart.

And that you find your way too.

You don't need an instrument
You are the instrument
Play.

BERNADETTE SOMERS

Amazing Grace *

I had a daughter named Grace, but she never made it to this world. Her heart was once beating, albeit slowly, but the sound of that beat was music to my ears.

She was ten weeks old and swimming in my waters, but her little feet never touched the ground. She remains lost in the moments that never got to be birthed. She is etched in my memory like a scar above my heart.

I had a daughter named Grace and she was amazing, just like the song.

I had really never encountered any major obstacles until I lost Grace. I fell pregnant easily with my first three children and never had difficulties conceiving. I somehow believed I had paid some karmic debt by navigating my way through unremitting morning sickness throughout each pregnancy. I think I believed that with every gain or gift, there had to be some setback.

My loss of Grace hit me hard.

I took to finding words in the form of writing poetry and songs to help me heal. I never shared my songs with anyone as they were intensely private, personal, vulnerable and raw. But they gave me a space and place into which I could pour the heaviness that I carried.

---

* Written by John Newton, 1772. Public domain. Quoted under Fair Use Act.

Becoming part of the 'miscarriage club' is not a membership I had ever considered.

Then along came Grace.

Amazing Grace.

Sadly, she was too amazing for this world and I'm certain she remains nestled in the warm and eternal embrace of my nan, Ellen, in spirit.

As I sat at my nan's funeral service lamenting this fact, I looked over to her coffin and saw the word Grace written on the hymn board behind it.

I needed no other reminder that they were together.

The loss is still hard to put in words, but I have tried to with this song, the first that I share in this book. My hope is that by opening up my heart to share it, that scar that Grace left will heal. I think that she lives on in her song, even if it's not that amazing. But it might be some form of healing for someone else that has experienced a loss like my Grace, and that would be amazing.

The song I wrote is called, *I See You.*

I SEE YOU

In the middle of the ocean, I see you
In the dawning of the morning, I see you
In the middle of my dreams now, I see you

In the faces of my children, I see you
In the middle of the playground, I see you
In the faces of angels, I see you

In my efforts to move forward, I remember you
In the quietness of my night time, I think of you
In the middle of a cool breeze, I feel you

You ask me to move forward, tell me to move forward
Where else can I move
You ask me to move forward
Where else can I move

In the middle of the ocean, I see you
In the middle of the forest, I see you
In the middle of my nightmare, I see you

I'm like an open wound
I just can't heal without you

BERNADETTE SOMERS

Re-reading the lyrics can feel like reopening an old wound, a wound felt collectively by millions all over the world who have unwittingly become members of this club of lost dreams.

I always felt as if the nursery walls were painted in my thoughts only minutes after discovering I was carrying a child. The paint was wet, and the smell was pungent. And we all know how the smell of fresh paint seeps into every corner and crack. That's what the loss of a pregnancy or loss of a child does; it seeps into every cell of your being, and the stain can never be erased.

So, when I sing, *I See You*, I remember my amazing Grace.

I sing to her, but I sing to myself as if I am the observer of me, wearing my sorrow.

I see you.

I see your pain.

I see every ounce of guilt, regret and remorse.

I see every vision of life with her still here.

I see her empty crib and her hollow room of loss.

I see it all.

But Grace, you were amazing, if only for ten weeks. You existed. You mattered.

And it matters to me that I honour your memory.

They say you are 'saving grace' when you do a good thing to redeem a negative experience. So, I kind of think this remembrance, this story, as saving my Grace.

May all the little lost babies be remembered as amazing and may they be seen as the lives that were here, if only for a glimpse. It matters for them to be seen.

May their heart beats live on in the heartbeats of their mothers. May my song honour their memory and may every grieving mother on this big revolving planet know that I see her too.

Your pain is seen.

And I send you love.

And I send you, grace.

Amazing grace.

Maybe I was blind to the loss of others before I lost Grace, but as the words of the song remind me, now I see.

I pray that my gift is my song and, as Elton John sang*, that this song is for you.

DOWNLOAD
'*I SEE YOU*'
ON SPOTIFY

---

* Written by Bernard J. P. Taupin and Elton John, 1970. Publisher: Songtrust Ave, Universal Music Publishing Group. Quoted under Fair Use Act.

All You Need is Love *

I have a morning practice. I sit and write. I think when I sit to write I find myself in the place between here and there. It's like the writing takes me to a place beyond my physical self. I think it's the bridge to my higher self, and I always find something in the words that make me stop and reflect.

It's not a lot different to writing a diary when I was young girl. It always felt good to write down my thoughts and feelings so that I could gain more understanding of them. Writing them down gave my thoughts some validity and permanence.

The challenge was always hiding my diary so that my siblings wouldn't read it. It's a bit the same with my journals. There are dozens and dozens of journals of daily written musings scattered all around my bedroom. And every one of them over the last six years of writing are incredibly precious and important to me. They hold so much wisdom and insight. Every time I revisit the words, they teach me so much.

When I sit to journal or write I find that I hear song lyrics and titles. They seem to arrive from somewhere out of the ether, and there is always some message for me in the words. In discussing this with others I have learnt that many others also hear song lyrics in

---

* Written by John Lennon and Paul McCartney, 1967. Publisher: Sony/ATV Music Publishing LLC. Quoted under Fair Use Act.

their thoughts and randomly find themselves singing lyrics from a song that has dropped in from somewhere.

There always seems to be a message encoded in the song and it always seems to arrive at just the right moment. Some people tell me they think they have found the song, but I actually believe it's the other way around. The song finds them. This is partly why I participate in a daily practice of writing. The words find me, not the other way around.

One particular morning I was writing, and I could hear the words, 'all you need is love.' These words felt like the most meaningful and complete sentence ever. As I looked at the words scribbled in my journal, I realised that the words were actually the song title of a famous Beatles song.

I started to wonder whether perhaps all of the famous Beatles' songs were channelled, whether they dropped in from some place that was eager to share some of its magic, just like *Let It Be* arrived in a dream to Paul.

I wondered if the words of their songs found them, not the other way around.

I decided to look up the words to *All You Need Is Love* in order to glean if there was any further message in the lyrics. A line in the lyrics found me, not the other way around. It's a line about being exactly where you are meant to be. This spoke very clearly to me.

As such, I realised that carving out a small piece of my morning to sit in my bedroom to write was exactly where I was meant to be. I think I understood that words could find me, songs could find me, if I made the time and the space to receive them. I just needed to make it a part of my day that I loved and honoured. I just needed to make it a priority. I just needed to understand that if I wished for life to whisper to me with words, I had to be found. I had to open up to the process and open my heart to receive the magic.

Not only do I now write every morning, but I am always looking to unpack the deeper meaning of the lyrics I hear. I look out for the cues and the subliminal messages. I think about what message might be encoded in a song that I find myself singing in the shower. I think about the song that plays in my mind before I drift off to sleep. I wonder about the song that is chosen for me to awake to by my radio alarm, or the song playing as I turn the ignition on in my car.

I think there are many ways for life to whisper guidance to me, and it knows that music will always have my attention. It knows that songs land with me, that I am tuned in, and the songs speak in a way I understand.

Now that life has got my attention through songs and music, I will never again be inattentive. To make that a priority, I think all I need is love. Love for the beat.

I know, like me, many of you feel you have an affinity with music. It's the language your heart understands, and you also find a deeper meaning in the songs and the lyrics.

I speak to so many people now who have their own special song with a message encoded in the lyrics. This makes me feel a special sense of connection to them. It makes me feel like we are all part of an orchestra, and all our beats, our hearts, are connected to play the symphony. I kind of feel like it's a weaving together of all hearts and the frequency of the beats.

And so, this chapter is a call out to us all. This is a reminder, 'All you need is love.'

This opens the heart and connects your beat to all other hearts. Then we all play the music together.

Life gave me an outline.
But music coloured me in.

BERNADETTE SOMERS

The Rose*

I send songs like sending flowers. I feel they have the same effect, something beautiful, thoughtful and loving. A musical gift, with a beat.

The problem with sending flowers is that they eventually wither and die. This in itself can be a reminder of the pain, loss and grief that the sender was acknowledging.

But songs don't die like flowers. The beat lives on and songs can continue to bring comfort long after the petals have fallen.

I send songs to those who are grieving. A desire to help is deeply embedded in me. It is part of being an empath and part of being connected to the beat. The songs help me process the emotions and pain I feel for the recipient. It feels like the thorn of a rose. It is a blessing and also a curse; feeling too much can sometimes be challenging.

I once sent a song called *Petals* to a mother I knew from the local primary school. She had posted a beautiful tribute to her baby girl on what would have been her 30th birthday. Her little girl was born premature and passed away. I could tell that her pain was still as raw as the day she experienced her loss. Although everyone's pain is a different burden to carry, my own loss helped me relate to that pain.

---

* Written by Amanda McBroom, 1980. Publisher: Warner Chappell Music, Inc. Quoted under Fair Use Act.

I think it has a lot to do with the beat.

As a mother, I felt deeply connected to the heartbeat of my two unborn babies' heartbeats. But I also feel for the fathers. I think as mothers, we are physically connected to that beat. And even though the fathers cannot feel that beat, they are still invested in it. The beat is not felt inside them, but the pain of the loss is.

Carrying that grief is a very difficult place to sit. It's similar to the in-between space of feeling someone else's grief as an empath. It's not your grief to carry but you still feel it.

So, I send songs to the mothers and the fathers. It's my way of making sense of things that will never fully make sense. I think I am indirectly trying to connect the mothers and the fathers back to the beat of their baby's heart. I like to believe that's the power of the beat. The beat makes sense, even if nothing else does.

On this particular day, I was sitting in my bedroom near my piano. I was feeling for the mother who was thirty years past the most painful day of her life. I thought of a rose and a rose bud. A bud doesn't really get the chance to open up and reveal all its beauty. I feel that's what it might feel like to lose a baby—not witnessing the petals.

I sat at my piano, pressed record on my phone and a song came in from somewhere. It arrived in a way that brought tears to my eyes as I cried tears for every parent that had experienced loss like this. I cried for my own losses, and for my amazing Grace.

I knew life was showing me that suffering felt by one is suffering felt by all in the big pool of our collective humanity. I knew that songs could heal me and could therefore help in the healing of others if I could just be brave enough to sing and share them.

I connected to her grief and wanted to send a song. I didn't send flowers, but I sent *Petals*.

And I healed a little part of me by endeavouring to heal a little part of her.

PETALS

Got a story to tell, a story of mine, about a little rose bud
Who didn't get to grow, didn't get to bloom
Didn't get to show her petals

Cause they took her as a bud
Cut her from my stem
And took her away from me

And I still smell her perfume
I still smell her perfume

It's a story of mine, it's a painful one
I miss her every day, I do
Didn't get to see her grow, didn't get to see her bloom
Didn't get to witness her petals

Cause they took her as a bud
Cut her from my stem
And took her away from me

Scatter her petals in the wind
Scatter her petals in the wind
Scatter her petals in the wind

My love
My love
My love

BERNADETTE SOMERS

For all the fathers who have experienced this loss, you may not have felt the beat inside you, but it was still part of you. You are still part of that beat, and that beat lives on in you. You were invested, and that still matters. With or without the birth, this made you a father. This beat mattered.

For all the mothers, you were connected to the beat, and that changed you. It made you a mother. And that you always remain, because you were connected to the beat. Your beat and your baby's heartbeat synced.

If your baby hadn't yet developed its beat, it is now in you. If your baby lost its beat, it is now in you. It stays with you, just like all the feelings of love and joy you felt with that beat get to stay. They stay with you, in you, in your heartbeat.

So, please let your heart open to this, let your heart beat for you and your babies, who live on through your beat.

Synced, eternally.

The beat continues.

I only recently bumped into the mother I sent *Petals* to. She told me a story. The daughter she went on to have after her loss had just gotten married. As she signed the wedding register, she chose the song, *The Rose* by Bette Midler to play in memory of her sister.

Songs and their beats hold such meaning for us. We create memories with them. And with them, we remember.

So, it is perfect that this chapter is named, *The Rose*. It is in memory of all the rose buds nestled amongst the precious memories, in the hearts of all their mothers.

DOWNLOAD
'PETALS'
ON SPOTIFY

Cry Me a River [*]

There are some days that we all need a good cry. You might have found that you have shed a tear or two reading chapters here in *Beat*. I certainly shed tears writing it. It brought me back to my heart and emotions that needed addressing.

Sometimes words and lyrics can return you to your heart to address what needs healing. They say that grief comes in waves. I kind of imagine every wave of grief sends our loved ones off to the light. Light travels in waves too, just like sound. So, waves of grief might actually serve that purpose—sending them off in waves of light.

I like to think that deep within us lies a well of grief, full to the brim of tears, a lifetime of tears for shedding. When we shed tears, we allow the walls of the well to dry, and stronger dry walls can better support the weight of grief. Grief is too heavy to carry. Crying releases some grief and also releases the heart. Crying a river of tears keeps the river in flow, keeps the water moving and releases the pressure. Crying can release the valve.

Hearts have valves too to prevent back-flow. If the blood doesn't move through, the whole circulatory system collapses. It is exactly the same with grief, it has to move through. It can't be stored forever,

---

[*] Written by Arthur Hamilton, 1953. Publisher: Cloud9, DistroKid, Warner Chappell Music, Inc. Quoted under Fair Use Act.

or the whole system collapses.

Songs can assist the grief to move through, and music plays a very important role in the release of emotion; it can facilitate the flow, a release. We know that water cleanses everything—so do tears—and we often feel better after a good cry.

Music can be seen as a conduit to allow emotion to flow which can help facilitate the healing process. Sometimes a song can play on the radio and have us in tears of remembrance, transporting us back to a time or place. There's a reason songs are chosen for memorial services and funerals, to honour the departed.

Music plays an integral part in honouring the fallen, the lost and the departed. They become their 'swan songs'. Some believe a swan sings a song just before it dies, a final performance before the curtain falls. That a beautiful creature like a swan would emit a beautiful sound as it departs seems fitting. I like to believe this is true.

Music and songs are part of the ceremony to honour the deceased, serving as a way for us to remember them. Songs allow us to entwine them with the melody, kind of like the swan song, holding the beauty. The melody lingers long after the last beat, and the memories of all those lost continue to play in the melody.

I once sat at my piano and allowed it to be the container for my grief. I let a song come through. I named it *Still with Me*, and its tune remains with me on the days I am missing a departed loved one. Both the questions and answers are found in the lyrics. And when I ask the question, I receive the same words as the answer: still with me.

If you need to release the pressure valve and shed some tears, my humble song might facilitate the flow. You might need to cry yourself a river and get lost in the flow. You might find it cathartic. You might find it dries the walls of your well and that might help you heal. Or you might just wish to read the words. You decide.

For me, it feels so still and quiet when I listen to the song. I don't even notice the shedding. The tears just release, as they are meant to, and that feeling stays with me.

I know the song is mine, but it feels as if it's for me, not my own words. It doesn't feel like it's me singing. It feels like it is all of us singing, connected to the beat and connected to the universal feelings of grief and loss.

No one escapes loss. It is the final curtain call, and we will all have our swan song. But there's beauty in that final song. There is beauty in its beat.

STILL WITH ME

You're with me, in sunlight
I feel you, do you feel me
In warm seas, starlight, quiet moments, cool breeze

You're with me, in shattered moments, teary outbursts
And the anger too
Cyclones, strong tides, in the rain, in the storm

Are you with me, am I with you still
Do you think of me, like I think of you
When I look out to the sea
Are you looking back at me
Am I in your thoughts like you're in mine

I'm angry you left me
I'm sad and I'm lonely
I don't understand why I'm not with you
I need you

In roses, butterflies, black birds and blue bells
In doves flying and owls standing guard
The kookaburra sings for you

I don't understand what's going on in my heart
I don't understand why grief tears me open but
I'm just hanging around and waiting for a sign from you
From you to show me that you are still with me
Are still with me, are still with me

Butterflies, hummingbirds, owls, flowers blooming
Dragonflies, daffodils, sunlight

BERNADETTE SOMERS

DOWNLOAD
'STILL WITH ME'
ON SPOTIFY

One Day at a Time *

If you have read my book *Yolk* you might be familiar with the story of Ellen, my nan, who lived to the incredible age of 100 years and 10 days. She was an important person in my life and has become, if possible, even more important after she has passed.

You see, I believe some people are paired up, a contract of sorts is signed, and even if one departs, they stay close in order to remain paired. There are many deeper spiritual ways to describe this, but I like to keep it simple. I like to describe it as a 'perfect pairing'.

Since my nan passed, she has inadvertently helped me in many ways. She helped me write a book, she helped me write a song, and she helped me understand the power of the beat.

I always knew we were kind of connected in a way when she was alive, but I never realised that this connection would strengthen when her heart was no longer beating. I always understood the power of music, but I wasn't fully aware of how music could come through a person.

On this particular day many years back, I had just returned home from visiting my nan at the special accommodation facility where she resided. Nan was frail, her body was failing her, and she

---

* Written by Sam Smith and Simon Aldred, 2017. Published by Naughty Words Limited, Stellar Songs Limited, Cherry Ghost Music Ltd. Quoted under Fair Use Act.

seemed to be despondent, realising that she had to wait for life's timing to decide her final breath. Despite the sharpness of her mind, her body was weakening.

I came home from the visit feeling sad and a bit helpless. I realised that none of us have any control over the departure date of our bodies from our souls and awaiting that departure date involved some unwelcome suffering of both mind and body.

I retreated to my bedroom, as I often do, because it is my place of solace. My piano is often on the receiving end of my emotions, and I often pour my heart out onto its keys. I sat at my piano, closed my eyes and put my fingers to the keys, unaware that a song was about to be birthed. I pressed record on my phone as I felt that something raw and real was happening and I might want to listen to it again to process it. I sang *Go to Sleep*.

GO TO SLEEP

It's alright now, it's alright
Go to sleep, go to sleep
It's alright now, it's alright
Go to sleep, go to sleep

You have fought your best
You are tired now
You have won the race
Now it's time to let go

Your body has failed
And your spirit is tired
It is time to go
We understand

It's alright now, it's alright
Go to sleep, go to sleep
It's alright now, it's alright
Go to sleep, go to sleep.

You're entitled to rest
You're entitled to leave
You have had enough
And your body is weak.

We know you have tried
To run a great race
Now go in peace
In God's great grace

It's alright now, it's alright
Go to sleep, go to sleep
It's alright now, it's alright
Go to sleep, go to sleep.

It's alright, it's alright
It's time to leave
It's time to leave.
It's alright now, it's alright
Go to sleep, go to sleep
It's alright now, it's alright
Go to sleep, if you need
In peace.

BERNADETTE SOMERS

I will never ever forget this moment when a song arrived from somewhere beyond me in perfectly imperfect form, words, tones, lyrics and rhythm.

To this day, I still listen to the original, raw, rough-edged recording and understand that this song was my healing. It was gifted to me to help me process my emotions.

Since that day all those years ago, many things have changed. Not only are songs channelled, but I have become the channel. I now hear not only songs in my head, but I also hear my nan. I never would have imagined that I would continue to remain connected to her in this way.

My gift is one of clairaudience, which means I can hear. I can hear more than what's in my mind, I can hear what's put into my mind through an open heart.

This is the simplest way to explain a very complex and mystical process. It isn't something that makes me any more special or gifted than anyone else.

I believe it's a gift we all can have if we truly listen. I think it's got a lot to do with the heart and its beat. I think it's got a lot to do with light in all forms. And light and sound are both forms of waves.

It makes perfect sense to me that I would be gifted hearing, and that this book would be my gift about hearing. The gift of sound in a beat in waves, and hopefully bringing light in waves.

A few years after my nan passed, I was preparing to run a Perfect Balance Wellness class. I taught classes that helped women achieve balance of mind, body and soul. I had run classes for many years at my home, and they were always combined with music. Since music is such an important part of my life, it was always going to play an important role in my work. At this stage, I was really wanting to change the classes and introduce more of a holistic approach. I wanted to add a meditation component to the end of the class and steer things in a different direction.

I was growing tired of just addressing the physical aspect of healing and wanted to delve deeper into the mind body connection. I felt that the classes were becoming more spiritual, but I was worried that the change to the feel of the classes might deter some women from continuing.

I knew I had to follow the direction of my heart, but it involved me stepping forward and revealing different aspects of myself. It was a challenging time full of change. I wasn't sure how much of the old me would be lost as I found the authentic me sitting underneath.

Before the class, I decided to sit and journal and chat to my nan. I thought she may have some wise words of counsel for me. I tend to write everything down that I hear without overthinking it. I do this from the 'heart'. It just flows out onto the page. I can then go back and read what's written and process the words with my 'head'.

This is what I wrote after I heard what my nan said: 'Bernadette, please don't worry, you are on your path. This was always meant to be your path, even from a very young girl. I could see it in you then and I can still see it in you now. Trust. I love you. Just take it one day at a time.'

The words were so calm, loving and reassuring.

My mother had given me one of my nan's cream woollen cardigans to keep after she had passed. The cardigan had become a beautiful and treasured possession of mine. My nan had a special name she gave me; she used to call me her treasured possession, and her cardigan became mine. Whenever I was missing Nan, I would get the cardigan and wrap myself around it. My nan also said on this particular day, 'Go and get my cardigan, wrap it around you and lie down on your mat, before the class starts. Then put your music on and please listen.'

The guidance was so clear and specific. So, I did exactly as she said. I laid down on my mat and put on the music from my class playlist of songs. The first song that randomly played on the playlist was a song by Sam Smith. I laid quietly listening to the words of the beautiful song and heard Sam Smith sing the words about taking it one day at a time. I was startled out of my peaceful state and jumped up off my mat to see what song was playing on the playlist. I instantly realised that the song had said the same words as my nan had said. This song was *One Day at a Time*.

The memory of this day is so vivid and so clearly etched in my mind and brings me immense comfort.

I think it is normal and human for the rational mind to doubt the mystical, the unexplainable, the non-sensical. My mind always tries to make me doubt. It is perhaps easier to deny than believe, but I have so many magical and mystical moments like this one happen to me and I know what I hear. I hear. It is clear to me. I don't doubt it, and my trust in it is my lifeline to all that matters. I hear it as clearly and as definitively as the beat of my own heart.

We don't control the beat of our own heart.
It happens for us. It beats for us.
I don't control the guidance I hear, the songs I hear.
They happen for me. They beat for me.

I will be eternally grateful for the gift of guidance and the gift of music, both a 'perfect pairing', just like my nan and me.

DOWNLOAD
'GO TO SLEEP'
ON SPOTIFY

Some people leave a footprint in the sand
That no matter how many tides roll in
Nothing washes it away

BERNADETTE SOMERS

The Power *

The lyrics of the song *The Power* by Vanessa Amorosi are close to my heart and close to my beat. This is because the lyrics sing to Mother Mary and they ask her to answer a prayer. The song invokes her power, and I think Mother Mary is a power.

I don't know whether you believe in a higher power, but I do. The relationship is between me and that power.

My relationship with religion has been like all relationships, it has had its ups and downs. I have become disillusioned with religion as I have grown older because I felt religion became less about the higher power and more about power. It became more about rules and regulations and less about love.

I always thought the power was in the love.

I always thought love was the higher power.

But many of the rules and regulations taught by my religion took away my power, my choices and my sovereignty.

And that took away my love for it.

Your religion might be different, but I can guarantee that your higher power is all about love. And love is found in the heart, right

---

* Written by Vanessa Amorosi, Paul Wiltshire, Mark Holden and Anthony Hicks, 2000. Publisher: Universal Music Publishing Group. Quoted under Fair Use Act.

next to the beat.

Despite my wavering love for religion, I have never wavered in my love for the feeling or consciousness of Mother Mary.

She is a power unto her own.

She is represented in many songs like *The Power*, with many of us singing her name and her praises in the melodies.

I believe Mother Mary represents maternal love, and the power of the love for the mother should never be diminished by religion. I tend to think some people put Mary in that religious basket, so to speak. But Mother Mary is also a feeling, a warmth, a representation of the deep, nurturing love, found in a mother. There is great power in seeing her as this.

Songs sung about Mother Mary or the feeling she evokes can speak ever so gently to us. They can remind us of being a child and being held by the mother. Mother Mary consciousness reminds me that the beat starts with a woman: that Mary birthed her son Jesus.

We are all here today because we grew from the mother, in her womb and from her heart, her blood and her beat. When we are in the womb, our needs are met, but not every person has their needs met outside of the womb.

Mothers are human, with individual capacities to meet the needs of their children. It might be because of how they themselves were mothered. Or it might be the result of multiple other factors and circumstances, some within and out of their control. Yet, many people end up carrying wounds in their hearts because their needs have not been fully met by their mothers, and the only way to help heal them is to open the heart.

I believe we can help ourselves to heal mother wounds by opening our hearts to access the feeling or consciousness of Mother Mary. I think we can draw on the feeling of her love. When we open our hearts to heal, we can connect back to the beat of our own hearts. I believe that beat can meet all of our needs. We can meet all

THE POWER

of our deeper needs if we come back to our hearts.

The heart is sacred, yet if you look at any art or images depicting the sacred heart, it has a wound. This is either an arrow piercing through the heart or a crown of thorns encapsulating it. There is always a wound, but I think that wound or piercing is where the heart opens up, where the light gets in through the wounds.

I know my heart has received wounds over its lifetime, but they have served a purpose. They have opened me up to a greater awareness and made me understand that all hearts have a choice to remain closed and wounded, or, through that entry point, welcome a new awareness. This is where the light enters.

When I look at historical art depicting Mother Mary, she is often showing her sacred heart, wounds and all. She lost her son: the greatest wound. But he rose again and the light returned.

I believe Mary is a figure to teach us that there is always light, even when there are wounds. You don't have to believe in her if that's not your faith, but you can believe in the feeling—a feeling about hearts and the capacity they have to hold light if you open them.

I believe Mother Mary is indeed the symbol of this. Remember, this chapter is not about religion, it's about hearts, mothers, wounds and healing. We all have all of these. The full spectrum is mandatory to the human experience.

Consequently, every song I hear that includes the words 'Mother Mary' holds great power for me. The song opens my heart. I connect my beat to the beat. I come back to my heart. This is how I open up to let in the light.

My wish is that this brings some healing to anyone carrying 'mother' wounds in their hearts. I hope you can feel the power of Mother Mary and the feeling of her love, and if that feels too hard to access, I hope that you can find access to your own heart and its beat and sync back into its power.

May the beat of the songs connect you back home to your heartbeat. And if you find any comfort in these words, I hope that you will receive more help by listening to my song that connects you to the feeling of Mother Mary. It might be just a feeling, but feelings hold so much power.

I tried to invoke Mother Mary or the feeling of her when I recorded this song. But the actual, original song came through spontaneously at a time when I was needing that feeling of love from the mother. It is simply called, 'Mother Mary'. That title holds its own power. I believe songs have great power and can land in our hearts and open a doorway or portal for connection. The listeners might not be aware that this is in fact happening but nonetheless feel a deep connection with the song. I believe songs land as they are meant to, and if my song lands with you, I am grateful and honoured, just as if my words in this book land with you, I am, again, grateful and honoured.

I have no control over what transpires, but I trust in a higher power. There is great power in that.

DOWNLOAD
'MOTHER MARY'
ON SPOTIFY

Life plays its song for you
But you write the lyrics

BERNADETTE SOMERS

A Sky Full of Stars [*]

I think that when we look to a sky full of stars, we can see many things. Perhaps we can see those who have left and also those who are ready to arrive. Perhaps we can also sense that things are soon to arrive. *Twinkle Twinkle Little Star* is a song sung by little children to teach them about stars. I know a baby girl that will one day sing this song, and it will be her song and her story. And I believe I looked to a sky full of stars and saw her impending arrival.

Many years ago, I stood in a gift shop mesmerised by a beautiful painting hanging on the wall. It was a painting of clouds in the sky and the art seemed to hold such magic, just like the stars.

I think that stars are magical and if you believe in the story of the birth of Jesus, you know that one bright star led three wise kings to his stable. If you don't believe in the story, you might still see the beauty in the symbolism of that star. You can find things of beauty in the sky, in its vastness. It's where I often look to; I look skyward to wonder, to make sense of all that seems unfathomable.

I discovered that the artist who painted the sky does the same. She uses this wonder and inspiration to bring through her art, and

---

[*] Written by Chris Martin, Guy Berryman, Jonathan Buckland, Tim Bergling and William Champion, 2014 Publisher: Sony/ATV Music Publishing LLC, Universal Music Publishing Group. Quoted under Fair Use Act.

the synchronicity that unfolded from our pairing is unfathomable.

After seeing the beautiful painting, I searched up the artist and followed her work on social media. This began a long love affair with her work, particularly of the art depicting the sky. I find wonder in the sky. She paints wonder from the sky.

This artist, who looked to the sky to bring in that magic, created that magic in me. It created the same kind of wonder. At this time, I had a half-written book and a strong feeling that this art somehow aligned with it. It seemed all unfathomable and full of wonder. I could visualise her art of the sky as the book cover, but I wondered how I could possibly make that happen. I guess I just tried to 'stay in the energy of believing it was possible.'

One day, on a whim and a prayer, I decided to call the artist and tell her about my vision. I remember saying that my name was Bernadette, that I loved her art, and I would love one day to put it on the cover of my unfinished book. The artist was so warm and welcoming and spoke to me like we were long, lost friends. And that is exactly what we became.

I believe that was always written in the stars. Her art went on to become the beautiful cover of my first book and our connection grew from that special bond.

As we became closer, she mentioned to me that she was ready to start a family and wanted to become a mother. I immediately felt in my heart that she was destined to become a mother, and I intuitively felt that, like a plane flying in the sky, it would soon land. I remember receiving guidance for her, telling her to metaphorically put the lights on the runway, as a baby was ready to land. But she had to be in 'the energy of believing it was possible', just as I did in order to birth my book.

After passing on the message, she shifted into believing it was all going to fall into place. And, as if it was all written in the stars, it began to. A sky full of stars holds all the energy of possibility.

Some weeks later, I was sitting to meditate and journal when I heard some words.

I heard, 'Pop the champagne, she's on her way.'

A little girl was on her way. I kept this to myself, as although I trust and believe in what I hear, I would never want to interfere with the hopes and dreams of those wanting them fulfilled.

At the time, my husband and I were wanting to change the fence around our house. So, we decided to go for a drive to look at fences. We ended up venturing very close to my friend's home. I decided to put a call through to her and she asked us to pop over. My husband said we should take something with us and not arrive empty handed, so he stopped at a bottle shop and purchased a bottle of champagne, and then we went to her home.

We were all chatting, and I remembered the guidance I had received earlier in the day. I knew it was important to stay in the feeling of believing things were possible, so I mentioned that I felt really positive for her. She told me she had a very strong feeling that she was going to have a baby girl. I then realised that my journal notes from the morning had mentioned, 'Pop the champagne, she's on her way.'

I realised that it had two meanings, both me going to her home to drink champagne and the baby girl being on her way too.

That was magic and that was wonder.

A few months later I was in the newsagency and I saw some pink wrapping paper etched with the words, Twinkle twinkle little star'.

I decided to purchase the wrapping paper with a feeling that it would one day, be used to wrap a birth gift for my friend's baby girl.

I called this baby, 'little star'.

Not long after this, my artist friend heard the first beat of her unborn baby girl's heart. She was pregnant with her 'little star'.

She is now the mother of a beloved baby girl, who landed into their beautiful family in divine timing. This baby girl reminds me that some things are destined and written in the stars.

This magical story reminds me of the words from Phil Collins song, *In the Air Tonight*.*

Sometimes we just have a feeling that something is 'in the air,' that something is coming. We look to the stars for answers, to confirm our knowingness. We look in wonder. We see the wonder.

Phil Collins knew what it was like to sync to the beat, and his song, *In the Air Tonight* has the most powerful drumbeat solo at the end. He also knew what it was like to connect with the 'unfathomable' and see the wonder. He has said he wrote the lyrics to his song spontaneously, using the same magic and wonder, and created a timeless song with a powerful beat. This beat continues on, and so does the wonder. I wonder if they both came from the stars.

Sometimes the words in a nursery rhyme can best explain the wonder. I believe that my friend's baby girl was always destined to have her own heartbeat. I believe the sound of that beat was always destined to fill her mother's heart with love. I believe the song *In the Air Tonight* was always destined to have its beat. And I believe the sound of that drum beat fills us all with wonder.

I feel very blessed to be part of the life of little star and her beautiful mother. I believe the sky, depicted in the art, indirectly led me to them both. Just like a sky full of stars.

---

* Written by Phil Collins, 1981. Publisher: Concord Music Publishing LLC. Quoted under Fair Use Act.

Sometimes when I close my eyes
I see stars
If I focus on them, they disappear
They just wish to be in the background
Like a guiding light
Guiding me home
I think they are my lucky stars
Made of my own star dust
Sending me light
Sending me love

BERNADETTE SOMERS

Heavy on My Heart [*]

Life without music feels heavy on my heart, and I am certain that singing opens up my heart. I always loved to sing, but when I was younger, I didn't have the courage and confidence to be a singer. I remember saying to my husband around 22 years ago that if I didn't pursue singing in my lifetime, I would die with regret. It was around the same time Anastacia hit the airwaves, shared her music with us, and welcomed us all to her truth.

I remember thinking that Anastacia, who sang *Heavy on My Heart*, epitomised everything that I was not. She was confident, courageous, sassy, and appeared to fully own her feminine power. I thought she represented a woman completely balanced in her masculine and feminine energy.

I didn't feel like Anastacia. I found it challenging to find my voice, and I have spent the better part of this millennium trying to overcome this challenge. Singing helped me to do this.

I know the soul part of me longed to sing, but my mind tried to talk me out of it and my body sabotaged the process. Singing in

---

[*] Written by Anastacia Newkirk and Billy Mann, 2004. Published by Kobalt Music Publishing Ltd., Universal Music Publishing Group. Quoted under Fair Use Act.

front of people made me crippled with fear—knee-shaking, throat-closing kind of fear.

I grew up attending karaoke competitions at the local pubs and found a way to get up and sing, but only after drinking some alcohol for courage.

I sang at my brother's wedding ceremony but made sure I remained hidden in the background when performing. The knee-shaking continued long after the performance.

It took me a long time to realise that some things in your life you sign up for. You sign up to get them in order to overcome them. Returning back to balance or harmony involves working through these challenges.

I think that harmony is not just about beautiful voices merging. It's a state of balance and equilibrium, in which everything is in perfect flow. It took me a long time to realise that I could work on the mind and body aspects of trying to stay in balance, but I had to also address that soul part of me that wanted to sing. I feel it was all about returning home to the beat, returning home to my heart and doing what I loved.

I always knew there was something intrinsically important about music and the beat for me, but I just didn't know how I could find my inner Anastacia to bring that aspect out.

One day I sent out a challenge. I called out to life and hoped that it was listening. I knew I could return to harmony if I could find the courage to sing to that harmony. I yelled out to whomever was listening, in whatever dimension, for what it was worth. *Okay I will do it. I will sing. I don't want to fear it any longer. Please make it happen.*

Life must have heard my voice. I think it was waiting for me to find it. I think it was amused because it knew that this was exactly what I had signed up for.

The next day there was a notice in my children's school newsletter about putting a band together. They were looking for parents interested in joining. They were looking for singers. The issue with asking for life to assist is that when it does, you can't ignore it. It is a gift, and you must accept it, as you ordered it.

So, I accepted. I joined the band as a back-up singer, and after a year of finding my feet, inadvertently became the lead singer. I still pinch myself to this day that I have overcome the knee-shaking, throat-closing nerves.

When things come down to the wire, you can find yourself facing a now or never, choose it or lose it moment. You are ushered towards the path that will help you overcome the things you signed up for. You have to go with the momentum, and you have to ignore the fear and the judgement. Judgement does not disappear, as people will always judge you. Some will judge you if you take your chance and some will judge you if you don't. There will be judgement no matter what you do or what path you take. The point is you still have to take your chance; you still have to walk your path. You have to follow the calling, in spite of the fear, in spite of the judgement. In spite of the spite.

Something I have learnt from singing is that you have the capacity to find all different aspects of you to bring forth. We are all, in fact, a big melting pot of different 'aspects' waiting to be accessed. We are told we can find the inner strength to channel or call on when we need it. We are told we can be anything we want to, if we have the self-belief. So, we all can channel the qualities, the aspects of ourselves from somewhere.

I would love to believe it is from the same 'source', the same 'somewhere' where my songs come from—that these things are waiting in the wings. And I truly believe once you tap into the source, it feels as if you have touched an angel's wings, just like Anastacia sings about.

I am not Anastacia, but I can now find that facet of myself that I need to draw on when I sing. It's not acting. It's embodying. It's drawing on the fullness of the abundance of reserves within. It feels like solar power. If we always have the sun, then we always have the power. I sometimes think we just need to see that sun's brilliance in ourselves to see the vastness of our own potential.

It kind of feels like sunlight now, when I am singing, and I go with that feeling. I still sing and I will always love it.

That is the truth. Welcome to my truth.

Life told me to stay tuned
Like I was waiting for something good to arrive
And I realised that life meant stay tuned
Stay in the frequency
That attracts the good
Stay tuned so you feel it has already arrived
And then I got it, the concept
And the good.

BERNADETTE SOMERS

Healing Hands

Have you ever thought that the hands are an extension of the heart? When you want to show love, do the things you love, or do things with love, you need your hands. When I want to write or play the piano, I need my hands. They are connected to my heart. And I can connect into the heart and send love through them.

A musician needs to use their hands to play an instrument. And singers often cannot perform without using their hands to convey the feeling of the lyrics. We use our hands to connect to the beat, whether by clicking our fingers or clapping our hands. I believe our hands are the expressive part of our hearts, so they have to be connected to the beat.

When a baby first learns to clap their hands, it is almost a coming together, or coming back to centre. It's the discovery of two individual working parts joining in unison, just like the hands and the heart.

It is something a child learns to do to show joy and to sync to the beat of music.

We bring our hands together in prayer and in a gesture of peace. Placing our hands on our hearts to feel the beat and connect back to ourselves is a powerful way to come back home.

I like to think of life, having hands and healing hands. I have an image or visual that brings me great peace and clarity. I like to think of myself holding onto life with two hands, feeling steady, safe and held. This is the feeling I get when I receive guidance, when I hear life whispering. I feel connected with both hands holding onto life as my support system, as my lifeline.

When I choose to pass on guidance by writing it, singing it or speaking it, I feel as if I loosen one hand from life in order to reach. I reach ever so carefully and gently so as not to upset my balance. I reach for someone else to share with them, to share what I hear. I like to think that my reach takes their hand and acts as a bridge back to life and all its whispers. It might connect them. It might not. I can only reach. I am reaching for their hand but after reading this, you will see, that I am also reaching for their heart.

Hearts and hands are connected. I can't ever control what my reach will achieve; it might help, it might not. I believe they need to have both their hands reaching back, and their hearts open to receive.

I will never, ever release both my hands from life in order to reach for someone else; this is something I cannot ever do because holding onto life and its guidance is my saving grace. And I need a life with grace. It is my self-preservation. This is how I stay in balance, making sure that I never deplete myself in order to reach for another. This stops me falling and prevents me from depleting my energy and my heart. I have to hold on with at least one hand to keep the gentle, continual supply running from life to me. I have to use one hand to reach and one to hold on.

I think that this applies to so much of my life and maybe yours too: releasing yet holding on and finding that balance. It is very much like the role of our hearts: receiving the blood in and pumping it out with the right pressure and sequencing, the right beat. Not too fast, not too slow, regulated, balanced.

So, my way of keeping afloat is this delicate balance of using my hands and my heart. Both connect me to life and connect me to its beat.

I hope this helps put my connection, life whispering and source into words. As my reach, life brings me words to write. As my reach, life brings me songs to sing. If I keep one hand holding onto life's hand, it will continue to help me. If I reach with my other hand, I get to write and sing. I get to do what I now believe I came here to do. All of this connects me to the beat.

You may understand this 'hands' metaphor from the feeling that is evoked from the beautiful song by Elvis Presley when he sings about taking his hands and his whole life too[*], like the two are both intrinsically entwined. Using my hands, my 'healing hands', is my reach, as my hands are an extension of my heart.

I hope I have reached. May we hold hands as our hearts beat together.

---

[*] *Can't Help Falling in Love*, written by George Weiss, Hugo Peretti and Luigi Creatore, 1961. Publisher: Universal Music Publishing Group. Quoted under Fair Use Act.

Staying Alive *

Staying Alive was a hit song by the Bee Gees, which was released for the movie, *Saturday Night Fever*. The song became the band's most famous song and remained at the top of the charts for over four weeks. It has a very distinctive beat.

I find it ironic and very symbolic that the beat of this song, *Staying Alive* is the exact beat we are encouraged to mimic when giving CPR. When the heart has stopped beating, and we need to resuscitate a person, we need to stay in the same beat of *Staying Alive*.

They say the human heart is about the size of both hands joined to form a fist. I always think of the fist in a forceful way; it applies force. Isn't it ironic that we need the hands to apply this force to reinstate the beat?

When life is 'going nowhere' and we need to help somebody, as the lyrics imply, we use this beat. It is recommended that when giving CPR we aim to give 100-120 chest compressions per minute. The American Health association encourages us to remember the beat of the song to help save a life.

A song might actually save a life. A beat might save a heartbeat. When the lead singer of The Fray wrote the song, *How to Save a*

---

* Written by Barry Alan Gibb, Maurice Ernest Gibb and Robin Hugh Gibb, 1977. Published by Universal Music Publishing Group, Warner Chappell Music, Inc. Quoted under Fair Use Act.

Life,* he would not have envisaged that a young man downloaded it from his computer just before he died in a car accident. The song became his tribute song at his funeral.

Songs have the power to change lives and maybe even save them. Songs might be in someone's thoughts just before they pass or playing as someone passes.

I have been told a beautiful story that my song *Go to Sleep*, which was written for my nan, was played in a nursing home as an elderly lady was close to passing. The song was meant to bring her comfort in her dying hours and send her off with the beat.

I cannot think of anything more beautiful: my song sent someone off to something new.

My beat was playing as her beat ceased to play.

While we might all wish we could stay alive, it's comforting to know that the music goes with us when we depart.

Staying Alive was only one of the iconic songs from Saturday Night Fever. Another was the immortal, *Symphony No. 5*, which was arguably one of Ludwig van Beethoven's finest pieces. The 5th symphony was composed by Beethoven at a period in history that represents the transition of one musical era to another: classical to romantic.

Beethoven was a man who could not hear the beat for a large part of his life. However, his deafness did not prevent him from composing music that continues to 'stay alive' in our hearts and minds. His music has transitioned through the years and stayed with us.

I think the beat does the same, it transitions even after we pass. And I think that all dimensions hear the beat, even the dimension

---

* Written by Isaac Slade and Joseph King, 2005. Publisher: Sony/ATV Music Publishing LLC, Warner Chappell Music, Inc. Quoted under Fair Use Act.

that we ascend to.

Beethoven is likened to Columbus in that he explored the sea of music. His music transitioned through the waves, and still lands on our shores today. His beat continues.

An 'ode' is the Greek word for song and is described as a lyrical poem. It also means a tribute to someone. Beethoven composed an *Ode to Joy*. I think it is incredibly fitting that his music still brings us joy. And I think it is fitting that this chapter is an ode or tribute to a man who freed the music so that it could live on in the beats of all our hearts.

He is remembered in the beat. And the beat keeps us all 'staying alive'.

I Got You Babe *

The famous song *I Got You Babe* by Sonny and Cher, has lyrics about wearing a ring. The song always reminds me about my own special ring gifted to me from my nan.

Many years ago, when I was a child, my parents took their first ever European holiday and left their seven children in the care of my grandparents, Ellen and Bob.

It was indeed a big ask for two older grandparents to mind seven children, but they looked after us all with much love and care, and my parents were very deserving of some time to themselves to travel overseas.

As a thankyou gift, my parents bought my nan a beautiful sapphire and diamond ring. She wore this ring for many years and only towards the end did she decide to part with it. As Nan was approaching her 100th birthday and she knew that she did not have much time left, she decided to pass on some of her treasured possessions.

I went to visit my nan just before my own family of 6 were about to leave on our first European holiday. My nan gave her ring to me. It was very fitting, and it seemed to be the gift that allowed me safe passage. I think it was also the gift that gave her safe passage.

---

* Written by Sonny Bono, 1965. Publisher: Warner Chappell Music, Inc., Wixen Music Publishing. Quoted under Fair Use Act.

I GOT YOU BABE

I believe the bequeathing of treasured possessions before someone dies is an act of surrendering to the inevitable in order to allow safe passage to the place that comes next, wherever that is.

My grandmother passed away seven months after passing on her ring to me. Whenever I wear this ring, I always feel close to her. I wear it to special family functions and celebrations so that a part of her remains present.

I have three sons and one daughter, and the lyrics in the song, *I Got You Babe*, feel like they are both from my nan to me, and from me to my daughter. I 'got' a babe, an only daughter, a flower amongst all of her brothers. I 'got' a special bond that will always remain with me, just like the bond I have with my nan.

Recently my daughter was ready to make her own trip overseas to Europe. I thought she should take Nan with her. I got her to wear my ring.

My nan was from a generation that really never got to travel the globe and experience the world like my family have experienced. So, it seemed fitting that my daughter should wear her ring. I feel the ring keeps my nan close but also keeps my daughter protected. Just like the words of *I Got You Babe*, the ring seems to carry that same feeling of reassurance: I've got you, you are safe, and I am with you.

My daughter has travelled to France and the UK in order to follow the beat: both the beat of her heart and the beat of the music. In her travels she has seen Dua Lipa in concert in Lyon, and Harry Styles in London.

Two of my favourite photos are of nan's ring in front of the Eiffel Tower and Big Ben. Nan was there for the beat.

The beat continues to connect us to people and places that create lifelong memories.

I have a camelia plant growing in my garden that was given to me in memory of my grandmother. It brings me flowers in the spring. Every time it blooms, I pick a flower and put it in a vase on my bedside table. The plant reminds me of the inevitable seasons of life, and that one day, we will all face our own winter.

The blooming of our daughters feels like their Spring, and it reminds me of their rite of passage: the right for our young to leave the nest and experience the wonders of our world.

Just like the circle of a ring, all things move full circle. Our children grow up, our grandparents and parents pass on, and we season through it all.

But the small tokens that are left behind, the flowers, the rings, the keepsakes and treasured possessions, keep our loved ones close through every season. They also help to keep their memories in our hearts, close to the beat.

Sometimes I look down at my hand wearing that full circle of my nan's ring. I see her hand. I see my daughter's hand. I see the hand of life reaching out to connect us all.

Candle in the Wind *

Just like a burning candle extinguished in the wind, life can be fleeting. *Candle in the Wind* is a song that honours Marilyn Munroe and was also sung as a tribute to Princess Diana. Two beautiful women who mattered.

I think our spirit is housed in our matter, and that is why we matter, regardless of how fleeting our lives are. We all matter. And songs can be a lasting tribute to those who still matter.

One day I was sitting at my piano, as I often do, and I was thinking about a young mother who had lost her life, along with her three children, at the hands of her ex-husband. She was a victim of domestic abuse. I felt that her life was extinguished, just like a candle in the wind, and that she, and indeed many others like her, needed a song to say that they mattered.

I thought about all the women all over the world that were fighting for their needs and rights.

So, I sang my song, or rather, it sang me. Either way, it mattered that I got it out, for all of those who mattered.

---

* Written by Bernie Taupin and Elton John, 1973. Publisher: Universal Music Publishing Group. Quoted under Fair Use Act.

MATTER

I thought I might try to put to words
All the things you didn't get to say
I thought I might try to be the voice of you
And tell the world, you matter

Because you didn't get your chance
They silenced you
You didn't get to find a way to
Speak your truth
You didn't get the time, or the voice to say
You matter, and you still do today

So, I sing for you, if you allow
I sing for us all now, I sing out loud
And I tell them all your truth
And I sing as you would say
You matter, and you still do today

I keep you in my thoughts
I won't melt you away
Your soul burns bright
No matter what they say

I hold you in my strength
And let the fires burn
For in the ashes, you will return
To say you matter
You still matter
You still matter today

Gone but not forgotten
If you're not forgotten, you're not gone
This is a song for generations
Who didn't find their voice
And a reminder for me to find mine

Because I matter, you matter
We all matter
I hear us sing, we matter, we matter
We all matter

You matter
You matter to me

BERNADETTE SOMERS

I sat at my piano, finished my song and cried. I cried for all who had gone before me, all who mattered. I believe they can still hear me, as sound is frequency, and we all come from sound—the sound of our beating hearts.

I sang for all because I know that one person's healing can contribute to everyone's healing. If I could sing and find my voice, they could find theirs in my song.

I don't think I quite understood this concept of healing, until I learnt more about sound healing. I believe sound healing is for all that 'hear', not just those who are 'here'. And if I can hear the voices of those who have gone before me, they can also hear me. So, they too can hear the sound.

Sound matters, songs matter, and it really matters to me that I am the voice of those who have gone before me, to honour them in sound and honour them in song.

I don't think I will ever underestimate the healing effect of the beat, of sound. Sound is medicine. This was confirmed to me only days after singing my song, *Matter*.

I was gifted a free spot at a beautiful sound meditation class run by a friend, a musical soul sister.

A few weeks earlier, she had an intuitive guidance reading with me, and her guidance was all revolving around the theme that she was ready to 'fly solo'. She was ready to branch out and start offering sound meditation classes on her own.

The essence of her guidance was that it was the right timing for her, and that sound was going to help so many people to heal. Life was guiding her to use sound for healing, just as it was guiding me.

As synchronicity would have it, on the morning of our session, she had posted on social media about a favourite song she listened to when she was 'flying solo' as a young adult, travelling around the world. The song she posted was called *Offshore* by Chicane.*

After our session together we realised that the album cover photo for this song was of a plane. A plane ready to fly. This all tied in with the resonance of her guidance.

So, I went to my friend's sound meditation class and laid down on my mat under a blanket so I could rest peacefully whilst listening to the sound of the singing bowls.

When I was in a deep, meditative space, I suddenly saw a very clear image of Princess Diana. She stepped forward and spoke very clearly. She said two very important words: 'I matter.'

I could not believe that she had said the words from my channelled song. I told my friend about this image straight after the class. We were both blown away. I went home that night and re-read the words to my song, and it felt as if every word would be exactly Diana's words.

I woke the next day to realise that it was the actual date of Princess Diana's 60th birthday and saw her image and heard her voice all over the news broadcasts for the day. It was exactly sixty years on from the birth of a special woman, a beautiful soul who still matters. A woman who wished to be remembered as the queen of the people's hearts.

It seems so fitting that she is honoured in a song about still mattering, even after she has passed. It matters that she is remembered as the queen of people's hearts because that makes her close to the beat—both in songs and in hearts.

Whether it be from listening to my song or to *Candle in the Wind*, we remember her. She lives on in the memories. Songs matter. She matters. And so do all those who have gone before us, even if their

---

* Written by: Nicholas Bracegirdle, Christopher Elstob, Richard Sullivan, Graham Dear and Louise Burton, 1996. Published by edel UK Records Ltd. Quoted under Fair Use Act.

time here on Earth was only as fleeting as a candle in the wind.

I would like to hope that finding my own voice to share my song *Matter* might make all those who have gone before me, still matter.

I would like to believe that the synchronicities that occurred did matter and were signs for me to share my story. I have faith that the words of this story matter.

This story remains their story and I am only one voice, but we are all a voice together. This can create a small ripple that becomes larger sound waves. This can make a difference. This can ensure that women are heard, that their voices are acknowledged, and those who have been silenced or denied a voice can continue to speak through the sound waves created by those who speak up for them.

If we join our voices together, nothing can ever extinguish their candles in the wind. To me, that matters most.

DOWNLOAD
'MATTER'
ON SPOTIFY

Let the music take you to the place
Where you remember
So that you can forget
Let the music take you to a place
Where you can forget
So that you can remember

BERNADETTE SOMERS

Never Tear Us Apart [*]

I see words as codes. I guess it has something to do with being a writer, but I look at words the same way I look at life: searching for the deeper meaning. I see words within words and receive different meanings from them. I often see that changing one mere letter of a word can change the whole meaning, quite dramatically. Like 'lovely' to 'lonely'.

I also notice the duality words and their meanings. I notice this in the lyrics of the song, *Never Tear Us Apart* written by Michael Hutchence of INXS. A tear from crying, or a tear something pulled apart. It makes me think that anything pulled apart might result in tears. Both types, both ways.

This song always reminds me of Michael and his lovely life that ended with tears, as he was torn from the lives of all who loved him.

Michael was gifted, and it must have been lovely to be that gifted. But perhaps being that gifted belies a certain loneliness, a type of 'stand out from the crowd' loneliness. I would have said that his life was lovely, but I am certain the ending was lonely.

Changing one letter changes it all. Life is a gift, gifted to us. It can be lovely, but for some, it can be lonely. Lonely enough for some

---

[*] Written by Andrew Charles Farriss and Michael Kelland Hutchence, 1987. Publisher: Universal Music Publishing Group, Warner Chappell Music, Inc.. Quoted under Fair Use Act.

to take the gift, decide it wasn't that lovely after all and end it.

My friend took his life, took the gift, and the result tore many people apart. I think it was because we all saw his life as lovely; we didn't see the cracks. We weren't aware of his struggles and the absolute angst he faced of deciding whether his gift—his life—was worth keeping.

Returning a gift or sending a gift back always seems like such a dishonour. And so does suicide: taking a life, returning the gift. But we may never understand how it feels. Perhaps if we did it wouldn't tear us apart so much.

For those left behind, a healing process begins, which is wrapped in many, many thick layers. The first and thickest layer to unwrap is making sense of how someone can return the gift, how someone deems their life is not worth living. For me, the healing process always involves music, and the music of my own 'tears' helps me to heal. The music makes me cry, but it doesn't tear me apart. It helps to heal me.

I wrote a song for my friend. I wouldn't have thought he would know about it, as I was just trying to process the grief, but I now know that he does. Just as Michael sang, death doesn't ever tear us apart, and I can hear my friend, and he hears the music. He's still connected to the beat.

I think when I was young, I liked to nestle my head into the chest of my mother so that I could hear her heart. The continual rhythmic beat of her heart made me feel safe and comforted. I know now that's what music does for me. It's the beat: the beat of the heart, the beat of the music, both drawing me in where it's safe to rest and heal.

So, my song brought me comfort at a time when I was lost for words. I think this is how people feel when they lose someone to suicide—lost for words. I thought I found some words in a song, but I realise that they found me right when I needed them. Maybe they weren't so lost, after all.

My wish is that the words and the song find you if you need them, if you too are feeling lost for words. I don't have the answers, I don't know why things tear us apart, I don't know why some return the gift, I only have my song. I guess it is my gift to you.

LONELY LIFE

Just a photograph of your face
In black and white, in colour, of you
It's all we've got to remember
It's all we've got to cling onto tonight

Because you took matters into your hands
You took a chance to end all of your pain
So you'd be free
We're left with the memory of your life
Oh lonely, lonely life
It was a lonely, lonely life

What were you thinking
What were you thinking
What were you thinking of

What were you thinking
What were you thinking
What were you thinking of

When you took matters into your hands
You took your chance to end all of your pain
So, you'd be free
We're left with the memory of your life
Oh, lonely lonely, life

It was a lovely lovely, lovely, life
But for you, a lonely lonely, lonely, life

BERNADETTE SOMERS

BEAT

One letter changes everything. Lonely to lovely. One second changes everything. Here to gone. Who has the right to decide? The one who is gifted.

Michael was gifted beyond measure. He left behind his music, his gift, and its beat to continue to gift us all. I think Michael had wings, just as his song reminds us, and so did my friend. I think maybe they didn't know why—that they were going to use them earlier than we all thought. They both flew to a place where nothing can ever tear us apart from them.

Another INXS song that speaks to me with its beat is *I Send a Message*. I think Michael continues to send a message through his songs. Messages definitely do get through if you open your heart and listen to the beat.

Michael left his music behind for us all, and I am leaving mine in the beat. Returning the gift, still leaves a gift, and that gift lives on. My songs come from a place where two worlds collide, just as Michael sang about.

Everyone can hear the beat there.

DOWNLOAD
'LONELY LIFE'
ON SPOTIFY

Sometimes a record looks all black, shiny and new.
But when it plays, it is scratched.
It cannot play as it should.

Sometimes people are really struggling to play.
Because of the scratches.
So, we must be kind
We must be tolerant
As the world still needs everyone's music

BERNADETTE SOMERS

Like a Virgin *

I have a very clear memory of being at school when I was in Grade 5 and my teacher was reading a story to the class about Mary being asked to be the mother of Jesus. I had received a beautiful children's bible as a gift and I had taken my book in to show my teacher. My teacher said she would like to read a particular story to all of the children. Still to this day, I distinctly remember the words from the story. And I remember the line of that story that my teacher chose not to read out loud.

As the story read, the angel was telling Mary that she was going to be the mother of baby Jesus.

'How can this be,
since I am a virgin?'†

I remember watching my teacher screw up her nose as she adjusted her glasses balanced delicately on the bridge of her nose.

I remember she briefly paused as she got to this line, looked

---

* Written by Billy Steinberg and Tom Kelly, 1984. Publisher: Sony/ATV Music Publishing LLC. Quoted under Fair Use Act.

† Luke 1:34, *New Revised Standard Version Bible* Copyright © 1989 by the Division of Christian Education of the National Council of the Churches of Christ in the United States of America.

down, read on and quickly turned the page. That afternoon, I took my beautiful book home and opened it up to the words that my teacher had omitted.

I knew what a virgin was, thanks to the naughty boys in Grade 4 who thought it was a great joke to ask the girls if they were a virgin. Those who didn't know the meaning would always answer 'no', to a chorus of laughter from the boys who had led them into their trap. I, on the other hand, would always answer 'yes', which would not give them the laughs they were anticipating.

I guess they thought I knew the meaning of the word, but I didn't. I thought that having a September birthday made you a virgin instead of a Virgoan. However, it was catalyst enough for me to search up the real meaning of the word.

I didn't feel there was any shame associated with the word virgin, until my teacher omitted it from the story. It is funny how our young minds are so impressionable and can so easily make some truth from an incident or event from our childhood.

From that day on, I always thought the word virgin had negative connotations to it, rather than it being a word depicting the most divine and pure figure of Mary.

When Madonna released her song, *Like a Virgin* in 1984, I seemed to be the only person shocked by its title. I remember watching the video clip playing on the television in front of my parents and being puzzled by their lack of reaction to it.

It was then I began to realise that I had been conditioned to see the word virgin as something you didn't say or you might be ridiculed—like the boys in Grade 4 ridiculed the girls. I had learnt it was something not to be spoken about, as if the word was cloaked in shame and secrecy. But I had it all wrong.

I believe that as a child, I had grown up being conditioned and stifled by all the rules of the Catholic Church, particularly the rule that stipulated all women were to remain virgins until they married.

There's great irony in a religious rule that denies love.

There's great irony in a religion that forbids an act of love—when God is love.

I now understand love differently, and no religion will ever deny me love again. I now understand that acts of love, where a heart beats next to another, entwined in love, is never, ever a bad thing. No religion should ever forbid love in any form between two beating hearts, regardless of colour, race, religion or gender. Hearts have their own intelligence and can choose who they wish to beat next to. They decide, not the church.

Denying love and asking that a woman remain a virgin is denying them their birthright to love in all forms. No institution, religion or law should ever interfere with a woman's right to receive love.

Like a Virgin is one of those songs that can get stuck on replay in your head, just like the outdated rules engrained in outdated religious codes. Stuck on replay until we sync to a new beat.

I will never omit a line from a book or a song that tells a whole story. I will never condone a rule that forbids a woman from freely writing her own story, pursuing all that makes her feel love, loved and give love in return.

A virgin, to me, now resembles something so sacred, pure and whole, like all women should be seen, heard and honoured.

So, this story, however small, cannot be omitted from this book. It is part of the whole. It's important in its own small way, just like every word in a story. All words tell your story, and this is part of mine.

You will always find your way
When life is your teacher
And love is your compass

BERNADETTE SOMERS

Beautiful *

Christina Aguilera sings a song entitled *Beautiful*. The lyrics of her song remind me that words are powerful: they can tear you down or lift you up. I hope that the words of this book lift you up. They are my words. But like everyone, I have my days where my own words and self-talk do, in fact, tear me down.

As the words of her song remind me, I have to remember that I am beautiful.

As the words of my own song remind me, a song I share with you here, I have to remember to love all my parts.

I was having a bad day, reverting back to old patterns in which my own words were bringing me down. I was judging myself and my weight. It's an old pattern of mine; I say old because I would like to think I have completely overcome it. But like many lessons, they keep returning until you have finally learnt them.

I have always had issues with judging my weight and scrutinising my body as the 'right' size.

I am a very normal weight and have been my entire life, but my default setting is to try to control this. I don't think I am alone with this issue, and I know that there are many who feel like me; that judge the image they see staring back at them in the mirror.

---

* Written by Linda Perry, 2002. Publisher: Sony/ATV Music Publishing LLC. Quoted under Fair Use Act.

I see it as a tragedy, spending a good part of my life not loving all my parts.

It's something I no longer want to do, and when I witness so many young women judging themselves and their weight, I want to assist. I think if I help them, I might save them from feeling how I felt as a younger woman.

I now understand that if I fear my body holding on to weight, she will hold on to that weight more tightly.

She responds to the fear I 'feed' her.

She wants to be fed with love, not fear.

I often think back to when this pattern of judgement started, probably with an off-the-cuff comment from my father saying, 'your bum looks big in that'.

And I made it my truth. I didn't have the awareness to understand that perhaps he was projecting his own issues with controlling his weight. Or perhaps given his mother was overweight, he didn't want his daughters to be. It doesn't really matter what the reason was, the issue is that it was his issue, but I spent many, many years, making it my issue.

I don't know why I was so susceptible to believing the opinions of others, but I've learnt from this. I have spent many recent years relearning how to trust my own opinions and find my own truth. This has been a big lesson, but a good one.

I think when I tune into my heart, into its beat, my heart tells me that this is not how it wants me to spend the rest of my life. I think about how the hearts of the morbidly obese and the severely anorexic can give up the beat after too much struggle.

It's a struggle
Yes it's a struggle
But I'm trying to love me
Do you love me

These are words from my song *Parts* and could be the words of my own heart speaking directly to me.

I sat at the piano on this challenging day where my words were bringing me down. I figuratively poured my heart out, as if I was emptying all that I had stored in it over most of my life. I poured out all that might be contributing to its struggle to keep the beat.

As my song came through, I realised that if I didn't learn to love all my parts, I could never ask or expect anyone else to. It had to start with me. I needed to stop searching for that missing 'part' that would make me feel whole. I needed to realise that it was a struggle searching for something outside of myself to make me feel whole. I was done with struggling.

The quest for love starts and ends with self. There's nothing else to find but ourselves. Maybe another person might help us to find love for ourselves, but my point is *we* have to do the finding. It's just like finding our pulse; you can search on the wrist, or put your fingers to your neck, you can question and stress out, and say 'I can't find it.' But it is always there. The search might take some time, but it is always there to be found. It's constant. It's the continuance of you. This pulse or beat means life. And life is meant to be full of love, is it not? And this love must encompass self-love otherwise the beat doesn't make sense. The beat brings life with all its parts, and all those parts must be loved, even the not-so-liked parts.

My song *Parts* came through with no warning or planning, and the lyrics are a reminder of the struggle I want to relinquish. If you have this struggle, my song is your song too. The way it comes through means it's for everyone that needs it. It comes from somewhere, and I think that somewhere is a place where we all belong and sync to the beat.

Love all your parts. They are beautiful.

PARTS

I'm not going to lie here, I'm a little confused
I don't really know how to be around you
I'm not sure if you like me the way I am
Or you want me to be something different

Can you please tell me, what you see in me
Am I funny, am I smart, am I pretty
What's the part, you most like in me

I'm trying to love all parts of me
Let me know which parts you like the best
I'm trying to love all parts of me
Can you tell me which part
You like the best

I'm not sure about me
I'm trying to find that self-love
Everyone talks about
It's a struggle, yes it's a struggle
But I'm trying to love me
Do you love me

I'm trying to love all my parts
Do you love all my parts too
Can you tell me which parts you like best
I will like them too
I'm struggling, struggling, struggling

Can you tell me what you like
Can you tell me what you might love one day
Can you tell me you love all the parts
Maybe then I will too
Maybe then I will too

Is that the secret I need
To know you love it
And then I can love it
But I don't think that's how it works
I think I need to find the love first
Not you not you not you
I think I need to find the love first
Not you not you not you just me

BERNADETTE SOMERS

BEAUTIFUL

I think the lesson is this: don't outsource your love. Find it within. Don't seek permission to find something in you that's loveable. Find it yourself first. Just like the beat of your pulse, it's there, waiting to be found. It just might be your life force. So go find it.

DOWNLOAD
'PARTS'
ON SPOTIFY

I am just an outline
And music colours me in.

BERNADETTE SOMERS

Miss Celie's Blues *

Sisters come in many forms and can be found in lots of places. I have two biological sisters, whom I love dearly, but I also belong to a sisterhood. It's full of soul sisters, and I have found them through opening up the door to my spiritual side. It felt like they were all waiting on the other side of that door.

My life feels so much richer with these women in it. Some are my musical soul sisters; they understand the resonance of the music. Some are my silly soul sisters; they understand that it's important to laugh and relax as we transform through the messiness of an awakening. Some are my most loved and loving soul sisters; they hold me through whatever I am going through, and I would hope that I do the same for them.

I have learnt that distance plays no part in the coming together of those who are meant to be united. My soul sisters are from all over the globe and there is always a sense that I have known them forever. I used to believe that there wasn't any room for more 'sisters' in my life, that my cup felt full.

But now I understand that there is always more space to be found in my heart, for more soul sisters. My cup and my heart can

---

*   Written by Quincy Jones, Lionel Richie and Rod Temperton, 1985. Publisher: Universal Music Publishing Group. Quoted under Fair Use Act.

be overflowing.

I have a soul sister who lives overseas. She actually meets the brief of all the different types of soul sisters: loving, musical and silly. I love to make her laugh because we both have the same sense of humour. She was unravelling some old layers and experiencing the shadow side of transformation. I decided to video myself singing and dancing to the song, *Miss Celie's Blues (Sister)*, to cheer her up.

This song from *The Colour Purple** gives me all the 'feels.' It reminds me of two of my loves: soul sisters and music.

The colour purple is also significant to me. Often when I see my grandfather Jim in spirit, he is smiling and holding a big bunch of purple flowers. Purple is a colour that represents spirituality and enlightenment, and if you are drawn to this colour, it may symbolise that you have had some sort of spiritual awakening in your lifetime.

So, the colour purple is a deeply emotive colour, a moving film, and the song *Miss Celie's Blues (Sister)* moves me. It also makes me move to its beat.

I think, somewhere within us, is a place or space where we store the 'blues.' I see the different meanings of the word. We talk about the blues as a musical genre, and as an emotional state, but I actually see the two aspects merged together. I think the music or the beat of the blues makes us want to move, not in a fast, phrenetic way, but more in a slow, releasing kind of way. It makes us want to move the stored blues.

I wonder whether the blues are stored in the heart, right next to the beat. Moving to a beat helps liberate our bodies of stored emotion or energy, yet we rarely recognise this. We understand that it makes us feel better or that our mood has lifted, but we don't often

---

*   Film directed by Steven Spielberg, Screenplay by Menno Meyjes, 1985. Based on *The Color Purple* by Alice Walker. Distributed by Warner Bros. Pictures

recognise how moving to the beat absolves much more. It releases the blues.

In the film, *The Colour Purple*, Miss Celie had the blues; she had stored pain, grief and trauma inside of her. In order to heal, these things must be released.

When I listen to *Miss Celie's Blues (Sister)*, I can't help but move to the music and 'shake my shimmy' as the lyrics say. The music and the movement make me feel as if I step into the beat of all of my soul sisters from all around the world, like we are all shimmying to the beat as a united force.

The feeling I get in my heart when I connect to the beat is the same feeling I get when I connect with the soulful, loving, enriching connections I've found with my soul sisters. These are women who know me at my deepest core and who know and understand the rhythm to my beat. Women who replenish, support and hold space for me to be my authentic self. Women who make me feel anything but blue. Women who make me feel the colour purple, the colour of spirituality.

I really like to believe that somehow the beat of our hearts helps us to find our soul sisters, and we get to hold those bonds close to our hearts, close to the beat.

So, if you are looking for your sisterhood, see this as a sign to release the blues, the deeper wounds and sadness that engulf your heart. Your heart needs to be open to reveal its beat, and then it can connect with other beats. It sends out its beat in waves, just like sadness comes in waves. But all waves move. Waves are meant to move through you. And so are your blues.

It is red that merges with blue to make purple, and red is the full vibrant colour of blood, pumping life force through our vessels.

You too are the vessel and blood pumps through you in waves, to the beat. Find whatever you need to help get things moving through you. Move, dance, cry, stretch, sing, yell, chant, shake. Do whatever it requires to move the stored blues in your body from your heart.

This will liberate you, the vessel, of all that has you stuck. Let it move through you like waves. Release your blues.

As Neil Diamond reminds us, all of us can sing a 'song, sung blue'.* We all have the blues, but we can release the blues with the beat. And the beat can heal us.

---

* *Song Sung Blue*, written by Neil Diamond, 1972. Publisher: Universal Music Publishing Group. Quoted under Fair Use Act.

Bridge over Troubled Water *

Some days I feel I see myself as an older, wiser woman: a silver girl with silver hair and a lifetime of wisdom carried in my stories. Unless I share them, unless I find the courage, that silver girl just sails on through life, never dropping an anchor.

I always believed that life was for a purpose, for a sense of meaning. I always thought that I was not meant to sail on through the waters, but that I was meant to lay some roots somewhere. I always felt as if there was more that I had to give, express, write and sing. I just needed to find the missing piece.

Then I found my bridge, one that lies between myself and my spirit. It's like a bridge that connects me to a channel that leads me to the sea. It's a pathway to the wisdoms of all that have gone before me that still wish to continue on through me. I believe all inspirations are channelled for a reason. They are meant to be in physical form, and that can only happen if it's 'through' someone. This allows the continuance of all things. Nothing ever ceases, everything lives on. Just like a bridge over troubled waters helps us get through, I believe the loving guidance of all that have gone before us can come through me.

---

* Written by Paul Simon, 1974. Publisher: Capitol CMG Publishing, Sony/ATV Music Publishing LLC, Universal Music Publishing Group. Quoted under Fair Use Act.

I just have to be open.

I believe that any of us can be a bridge to this wisdom, guidance and inspiration, if we open our hearts. When I decided to be open, I was able to become the bridge, and pass on the guidance from departed loved ones.

A few years back, I was called to be the bridge between a daughter and her departed father. I needed to pass on a message that would be her bridge of hope. This beautiful woman had undergone a challenging road to becoming a mother, and her father wanted to give her hope that she would soon carry a child.

During the reading, I was encouraged by the father to draw a map of Greece, as the father was showing me a particular area on the map. Though my geography and my map drawing are fairly underwhelming, I was able to illustrate the specific area that the father was pointing out to his daughter. The father was born in Greece himself and was pointing to a town that I was not aware of but was able to name after hearing him say it. The town was called Messenia.

At the time, both the daughter and I were not aware of the significance of why the father was showing us this location in Greece. But we both understood that it was in reference to the bridge of hope he was giving to his daughter—that she would soon become a mother.

Less than two years later, this woman travelled to Greece to receive a donor egg for her IVF process. She was able to finally fall pregnant and is now the mother of a beautiful baby girl. She strongly believes that the donor egg came from a woman living in that area of Greece, near Messenia, where her father mentioned. She also knows that the entrance to this town bears an ancient bridge, which is an important landmark of the history of the town. That bridge tells a story. It represents an important time.

I really feel that this chapter tells a story and represents an important time too. It represents the bridge of hope over troubled water. This bridge between spirit and us can bring hope, and I can be that bridge.

I just have to be open.

During her pregnancy, this beautiful woman would often catch herself tapping her finger over her own belly button. She tapped like this whenever she felt a little anxious about the pregnancy. It was almost as if she was conveying a beat to her unborn daughter, using it as a bridge of communication. It was almost like morse code. She would always find her beat would be much faster than her own pulse and realised that she was syncing to the faster heartbeat of her baby girl. She tapped her finger to a beat, to connect with her baby's heart, to tell her it was all going to be okay. She used the beat as a bridge, using it to link two hearts as one.

I think that I did the same. I acted as a bridge, linking a father to his daughter. I linked two hearts as one. And although the father's heart no longer beats, his message of hope was still conveyed through my own heart, through my beat. I just had to be open.

I would like to believe that passing on this message from a father to his girl, helped to ease her mind. I hope it gave her hope.

I hope that by being 'open' in this story and this book that the beat might help you to open your heart. When your heart is open, all things can come to you through that bridge of hope.

They say when you have a 'heart to heart,' you communicate honestly and openly. May this be my 'heart to heart' story to you.

I now have such a beautiful open feeling in my heart whenever I listen to the song, *Bridge over Troubled Water*. I think there is an exquisite harmony found between the voices of both Simon and Garfunkel—a perfect pairing. I think both voices were needed to best convey the message in the song. And I believe that both voices, the departed father and my own, were needed to best convey the message.

I need hope too. I hope that I will always have the courage to be the bridge when others need hope too. Sometimes it is hard to lay myself down to be the bridge. Not everyone believes in a bridge. Not everyone has hope.

But I hope to lay myself down for those that do. May that always be enough.

Bohemian Rhapsody *

The song *Bohemian Rhapsody* is forever etched in my memory. It was the last song played on the dancefloor at my wedding. My family, who all love to dance, had gathered in a circle. It is a bit of a family trait to sing a song whilst motioning or demonstrating the lyrics. This is best done in circle formation so that every person can laugh at each other's actions. The laughter and fun we have when music is playing and we are dancing to the beat is probably one of the things I love most about my family.

I think this thing we do as a family is perhaps a little unconventional, just like the song *Bohemian Rhapsody*. It was also probably quite unconventional for the bride to be thrusting her veiled head into the circle as the song rose to its rock beat finale.

It was a different way to finish our wedding ceremony, but it is one of my fondest memories and my favourite song. The beat of the song always transports me back to that day.

Bohemian Rhapsody is an unconventional song; its composition is a blend of operatic, hard rock and ballad. It is free flowing and unusually long. It's a little offbeat, but because of its uniqueness, it is one of the most celebrated, popular and successful songs of all time. *Bohemian Rhapsody* was a combination of three different songs that

---

* Written by Freddie Mercury, 1975. Publisher: Sony/ATV Music Publishing LLC. Quoted under Fair Use Act.

Freddy Mercury had written, yet he never fully divulged the actual meaning of the lyrics to this song.

It remains a little different and unconventional. In fact, if we look into the meaning of the title, we realise that bohemian refers to a socially unconventional person. 'Rhapsody' means a miscellaneous collection.

I think *Bohemian Rhapsody* is as unique as Freddy Mercury was. I believe he and his song are a reminder to us all to celebrate uniqueness.

I believe many people 'march to the beat' of a different drum. Some people feel different, out of rhythm to the standard beat, out of sync to the beat on the street. Some can feel 'wired' to an unconventional beat, they feel they don't quite fit in or conform. Some days, I know exactly how that feels.

Coming to terms with my own unconventional parts—my spiritual parts—has often made me feel a bit different. I didn't feel like the old me after my spiritual awakening. I felt as if I had unravelled into something that didn't quite resemble the old me, but ironically felt much more like the real me. I just felt different, and it took me a few years to acknowledge, accept and embody all aspects of me in order to feel whole.

I was contemplating this and thinking about a friend who was navigating parenting her son who was feeling a bit different from his peers. I sat at my piano and my song, *Differentt* came out. It was even spelt differently.

I knew there were various shades of 'different'. It might be not fitting the stereotype or conventions or feeling grounded in one's mental state. I think there's a certain type of lingering anxiety that attaches itself to feelings of being different. It might feel like struggling to find the right tempo or beat when singing a song. It might feel like playing an instrument in an orchestra and knowing that you are the only one out of time to the beat.

BOHEMIAN RHAPSODY

I think I wanted to find the words in a song to give space to people who feel different so they can realise that maybe they aren't. Because, if I could I articulate the feelings in my song—that someone else is like them—then they aren't so different after all. Same, same, but different.

I know it's a hopeful intention, but I think if you 'hope for the best' sometimes the 'best' arrives. I guess it's a hope that the beat might connect us all so none of us feel different.

If you fill a room with hundreds of metronomes holding different beats, eventually they will all sync to the one beat. I believe our hearts can do the same, and I believe we have only touched on the incredible intelligence of the heart. I believe our hearts can all sync to one universal beat. That is worth hoping for.

DIFFERENTT

I woke up today feeling different from you
I woke up today feeling different from me
I'm trying to lift my vibe and change my energy energy for you
I woke up today feeling different, different, different.

Is that ok for you for me to be not ok not ok is that ok
Is that ok if I don't feel ok I'm not ok I'm not ok

I woke up today I'm feeling different from you
I woke up today feeling different from me
Please don't stress out, don't stress me out
Don't stress me out, don't stress out

I wake up each day I'm feeling different different different
I'm waking up each day feeling different different
I know you want me to feel better
So you feel better better if I am better better
I'm not better, you need to feel better if I'm not better
I can't be better for you

I'm different, I'm different
Can that be ok ok
Can you not stress out
Can you not make a scene
I don't want to be seen, don't be seen, don't make a scene

I'm not ok is that ok
I'm getting better in my own time
Can you not try to make me better better
It's not better better
I'll get better when I'm better
I woke up today not feeling like myself
Do I like myself
Do you like me, will you like me
If I'm not like you
Will you like me, can you like me
I'm a little different different
Different different
Different

BERNADETTE SOMERS

BEAT

May we all strive to find and hold the beat with all who are different.

DOWNLOAD
'DIFFERENTT'
ON SPOTIFY

Read All About It *

If there was ever a song that would be my own personal anthem, it would be this song *Read All About It* by Emeli Sandé. This song pulls on my heartstrings and stirs my emotions. I would like to believe that it's something that music can do, not just emotionally, but anatomically.

The heartstrings are thought to be the tissues that support the heart, the strong fibrous connections between the valves and muscles. They connect to the heart—and so do emotional songs. It is because of this connection that our hearts can open.

I haven't met the singer of this song, but I have a feeling that she would be a musical soul sister and that she would resonate with *Beat*.

She sings to us to read all about it in her song and I write to you to sing all about it in my book. I think we both have the same message, paired in word and song.

I am an open book. I have remained an open book in this book so that you can read all about it. I am not afraid. I believe there is so much that we are yet to fully understand about our world, other dimensions, our hearts and our minds. I believe we can learn more and open our minds, when we can 'read all about it'.

But someone has to go first and write. As Emeli sings, how can

---

* Written by Emeli Sandé and Shahid Khan, 2012. Publisher: Sony/ATV Music Publishing LLC. Quoted under Fair Use Act.

any of us learn from each other if we can't hear each other's songs?

My brother took a video of his son when he was about 3 years old. He was pretending to play a guitar and singing along to the song *Baby Did a Bad Bad Thing*.* It is beautiful and funny to watch this video and it makes me wonder whether my nephew was copying what he had seen the singer do or whether he was embodying it. Was it innate in him or was he just acting? I tend to believe that it was inherent. There is something beautiful about witnessing children sing or dance without any fear or inhibition.

It is sad that, somewhere along the way, we learn to shut down that childlike quality of our personalities as we become adults. I always believe the things that children express are innate and meant to be expressed. I think there are many signs to tune into that can be used to guide children towards the things that will fill their hearts as adults.

My nephew is now the lead singer in a band, and I believe he was inspired to use his voice for self-expression. The hard part is actually overcoming the fear, doubt and insecurity in order to be self-expressed.

If there could be only one message that could be taken from this book, it would be to come back to the heart and do what you love.

If music moves you, it is pulling on your 'heartstrings'. It's having an emotional and physical response. I find that music aims to emotionally and physically move you to take action and express what's within you.

And if music and singing feel that they call you and you feel part of that 'club,' then it is something that is innate within you. This indicates that your life is meant to be spent connecting to the beat,

---

* Written by Chris Isaak, 1995. Publisher: Warner Chappell Music, Inc. Quoted under Fair Use Act.

both the music and your own heart.

Singing is only one way to express yourself. Playing an instrument and creating music is another. Writing words that become lyrics is another.

There are many ways to be called home to what you innately love, but you can't waste your days living in fear of doing the very thing that you were destined to do.

You are the instrument, ready to be played. You just have to let it play through you.

This is the book for you to 'read all about it': the process of channelling what is meant to come through you.

Think of this: imagine a beautiful, perfectly crafted instrument sitting in the corner of a room. Never played. Never utilised. Never able to show what could come through its strings or keys. You are that instrument. How you sound when you play is really not the point. It is the expression of what is innate in you that brings you back home to your heart, to the beat.

It is never too late to learn how to play. Life is a playground, and you are that child meant to be doing what you love with wild abandon and no fear.

I will sing with you and for you, as I have done so in this book. I am not afraid, and neither should you be.

If I can do it, so can you. Join in the beat.

My Way [*]

I once was doing an intuitive reading for a young father. This lovely man was feeling ambivalent about his role as a father to his two sons. He had lost his own father several years earlier and was very much missing the presence of his father in this life. His father was of the ilk of so many others of that generation. He was the hardworking, breadwinner of the family in which there were many children and many mouths to feed.

His idea of being an honourable man and father was to work hard to pay the bills. This meant that he was at work more than at home which came at a cost of not always being available and present to meet the emotional needs of his sons. However, this was often deemed as the role of the mother. *Men didn't want weak, needy sons.* They were force fed on a diet of tough love.

This was how it was done back then, and most people seemed to get by. Or did they?

We are all very much a product of the conditioning of our younger years. Some of the patterns we learn are favourable for growth and some are not. It requires an awareness to unpack these issues and discern whether to repeat a learned pattern or change it.

---

[*] Written by Claude Francois, Gilles Thibaut, Jacques Revaux and Paul Anka, 1969. Publisher: BMG Rights Management, Cloud9, Concord Music Publishing LLC, Jeune Musique. Quoted under Fair Use Act.

We have a choice to do it our own way. Where we get caught up and confused is when we believe it is a dishonour to those role models in our lives if we do it differently. This was the dilemma my client faced. He was torn between being the kind of father he wanted to be and being a father like his own.

Life had given this man two sons and two opportunities to set the record straight and do things his way. One son was needing more from his father; he was emotional and sensitive and not of type who would be able to properly digest tough love. The other son did not appear to have the same sensitivities, but it made the father consider that just because he didn't identify as needing something, it didn't necessarily mean he wouldn't like to receive it.

This made him re-consider his own childhood, and that just because his father didn't provide the emotional support, didn't mean that he himself, wouldn't have liked to receive it. This was okay and safe to admit, and in no way dishonoured his father's memory.

This kind of inward soul searching can find answers, facilitated further through counselling and guidance. But when the message comes straight from the father, it is deeply heard. The father's message to his son was this:

> 'Son, I did my best, to the best of my capacity and I didn't get everything right. I see now that there were areas where I could and should have been more there for you. I am sorry. I am here for you now. You will honour me by being the kind of father you wish to be for your boys. That would make me so proud. That honours my memory. I am proud to raise a son who loves me but understands that it's important to do things his way. I did things "my way" and so should you.
> I love you,
> Dad.'

Paternal love runs deep through the veins of sons, and often men believe the best way to honour their dad is to do things the same way as their fathers did. Men can put their father's memory high on a pedestal. But pedestals can be unstable things; the higher you place things, the more things can topple off, including outdated teachings and stereotypes.

Outdated. Is the song *My Way* ever going to be outdated? I doubt it. Because it relays a very important message that men need to hear. It doesn't really matter how you get to the destination, so long as all the learnings along the way enhance the journey.

If you stubbornly do things your way, you might find the road is fraught with obstacles. If you resolve to do it your way despite the obstacles, you might find the road becomes easier because you show yourself your own persistence and determination.

If you do things someone else's way, you might always come to a fork in the road where life urges you to go your own way. This might be your sign to take a different path and be autonomous.

There are many ways to travel, and whichever way you go will indeed become your way.

Life is a journey in which we are all navigating our way forward, inch by inch, step by step, day by day, with no assurances, only hope and faith. But this is the only way forward, so you might as well make that way yours.

For those who need permission to do things your own way, life gives it to you. As life was gifted to you to use the gift as you choose. I believe this is the deeper message conveyed in Frank Sinatra's song. If you need permission from departed loved ones, the consensus and the chorus of angelic voices all sing a resounding *yes*.

If you need to tune into their guidance, their support, their ongoing love, just open your heart. They connect through your heart, right next to the beat. They remain constant in their love, just like the constant beat that brings you life.

Use this life that is gifted to you and do it your way.

The Way We Were [*]

Anyone who knows me well will know that *The Way We Were* is a favourite song of mine and has been since I was a young girl. I think I have always loved an emotional song.

It was released in the 1970s, around the same time that I was in primary school. I think melancholic songs have always touched my heart in a way that leaves a mark.

I have several memories of singing this song in a Parisian bar while travelling as a young woman and in a singing concert while pregnant with my daughter. I think my daughter likes and relates to the song as well because she would have heard me singing it from the womb.

I think that memories can light the corners of our minds, as the song implies. I believe memories carry light and I believe that our departed loved ones stay close if they are in our memories.

They say people are gone but not forgotten. Well, I believe if they are not forgotten, they are not gone.

Memories can bring light to the corners of our mind. But I also understand that for some people, memories are very painful.

Around the time of the song's release, a friend of mine lost a

---

[*] Written by Alan Bergman, Marilyn Bergman and Marvin Hamlisch, 1974. Publisher: Sony/ATV Music Publishing LLC, Tratore. Quoted under Fair Use Act.

family member in a tragic accident. I remember the way the family was before the accident and the way they were after. They were irrevocably changed but their external way of coping with their grief appeared to be to continue on as if nothing had changed. Yet I know internally, their grief would have been immense.

The family member that tragically passed was rarely spoken of. It was as if he, and all the years of his life, were extinguished, memories and all.

I grappled with this as a young child. I thought it was good to remember those who had existed, if only for a short time. I still do, to this day. I believe all lives mattered—and matter—and I wrote my song about it to honour this sentiment.

I always thought that if you weren't forgotten, you weren't gone. So, I felt deep sadness for this family. But the sadness I felt for the departed family member was deeper. He was not being spoken of or talked about. He and his memory were shut away in a closed vault of grief.

I am not an expert on navigating grief, and I am in no way suggesting that the family were wrong in how they managed their tragedy. I believe grief is a process and there might not be any right or wrong way to navigate it.

But what I now know as a medium is that our departed loved ones can stay close by. They can help us by providing light and guidance. Their memories can light the corners of our mind and help us to open our hearts to release the stored grief. They are still with us, not in a physical sense, but in an energetic sense. It upsets me when departed loved ones are denied this access because our grief prevents us from remembering them, the way they were.

I think my book and my songs are about honouring the memories in order to release the heart of the burden of storing grief. I realise my songs shared with you are sad ones, but I believe they are healing. And I think whatever we store away, under the carpet of our minds, can slowly erode us from the inside out.

Everything has to move through. Even grief. Hiding it, denying it or storing it doesn't help the heart. We've heard of people dying of a broken heart. It can all be too much to carry.

So, in my own way, this chapter is an ode to my own memory of a beautiful person who existed for a short time and then left. But I believe he remains in the memories, and he is gently and respectfully interwoven into this story. As I have 'memories' of the way he was, and my memories aren't as painful to remember.

I hope this story honours him and his memory.

They say gone but not forgotten
I say if not forgotten, then not gone

BERNADETTE SOMERS

Sing *

Sing was a song written for the iconic children's television show *Sesame Street*† but it became more well known when sung by The Carpenters in 1973. It has a simple message to encourage us all to sing.

Humans are not the only species that like to sing. Animals also sing, whether it be to communicate, attract a mate or share their location. However, it is thought that perhaps birds and whales actually sing for the joy of it.

I have always had a strong affinity with birds; I believe they are messengers and I have written many stories about birds in my book *Yolk*. I wonder if I also love birds because they sing.

The whale and its unique song also hold a very special place in my heart. Whales are able to produce a melody that can travel 10,000 miles through the water. They have even been observed singing when they have lost a loved one, a fact that makes me love them even more. When I have lost someone, I do this too.

It is mainly the humpback and blue whales that sing, but I

---

* Written by Joe Raposo, 1971. Publisher: The Joe Raposo Music Group, Inc Quoted under Fair Use Act.
† Television series created by Joan Ganz Cooney and Lloyd Morrisett Jr., 1969-present. Distributed by Sesame Workshop (formerly Children's Television Workshop).

particularly love the blue whale because it is the largest mammal ever to exist and has the biggest heart of all creatures. I would love to believe that this beautiful animal sings because it possesses a big, beautiful heart.

I would love to believe that the two things go hand in hand. So, I wanted to honour the whale's song in a book about music and hearts. A heart that big must emit a powerful beat.

If we know that our hearts have their own intelligence and cellular memory, then I believe that whales must have a lifetime of intelligence stored in their huge hearts. They say that when you look into the eyes of a whale, you are irrevocably changed. It's said to feel as if the whole world, all its secrets and wisdom, is looking straight back at you. Seeing 'eye to eye' is a connection, just like being 'heart to heart,' is communicating something important. I think that when we see 'eye to eye' with a whale, we understand that we are more connected than we realise. I think our hearts connect us. The beat connects us.

I think that the eyes are a channel straight to the heart. The enormity of the whale's heart makes this 'eye to eye' connection so monumental. I would like to believe in the ability of the whale's heart to communicate to us through sight.

We know that the eye processes vision through light, we know light travels in waves, and the sound of our heartbeat is waves. So, it makes sense to my heart that creatures that reside in the waves are connected to them and that communication can occur through them. Light. Sound. Water. All in waves.

This may sound unscientific and merely poetic, but I believe we still have much to discover about our connections to each other. My connection to the other side shows me that all things are possible. If my small heart draws me towards the beautiful whales of the ocean, then perhaps there is connection there.

SING

They say that whales not only sing but also breach to communicate. They breach out of the water and create waves. They breach up towards the light. They create waves and move towards the light. It seems to me that they are showcasing their abilities, shining their light, if you will. Anyone who has watched a whale breach would agree that it is a sight to behold. I believe it is only when these beautiful creatures breach and come to the surface that we can see 'eye to eye'. We witness their majesty and their place in our oceans—their home.

Whales are very symbolic in our history. Spiritual philosophy teaches of a time in ancient history where heaven was on Earth, just as Belinda Carlisle sings in the song, *Heaven is a Place on Earth*.*

This lost continent was named Lemuria and the people who lived there lived in harmony. Lemurians had a very strong connection to the water and all marine animals, especially the whales. In Māori folklore, there are stories of an ancestor named Paikea, who was said to be saved from danger by being carried to safety on the back of a large whale. There are countless other stories and bible references that illustrate the importance of this magnificent animal.

Whales appeared over 50 million years ago before man existed, so they carry a cellular memory in their hearts that is far greater and wiser than our own. I believe this is part of why whales remain close to our hearts. There are many people who feel a strong connection to the water; they wish to live by the sea or feel the desire to immerse themselves in the water. There are stirrings in the hearts of many who feel this resonance to the water and to all the lifeforms that inhabit it. And there are many people like me who are drawn to whales. They sense their intelligence. They resonate with their song.

---

* Written by Ellen Shipley and Richard W. Nowels, 1987. Publisher: BMG Rights Management, Spirit Music Group. Quoted under Fair Use Act.

I think the Beatles song, *Octopus's Garden** sums up the sentiment of feeling at one with the ocean or sea. It can feel safe like home.

I love how waves wash up on the shore and bring new things to land. I think that my musings in this book might do the same: allow new thoughts to land. They might stir your heart. The music might create sound waves that open your mind and your heart. You might realise that you are on land where you belong, next to the ocean where the whales also belong.

Every living being has their rightful home, and all is in order, all is in resonance. This is how I believe all things should be.

I hope that one day, I can look into the eyes of a whale and understand all of the mysteries of this beautiful creature as it imparts all of its wisdom about our home: both land and ocean. But until that time, I will enjoy listening to its song and enjoy the beat.

---

* Written by Richard Starkey, 1969. Publisher: BMG Rights Management. Quoted under Fair Use Act.

If you stretch your heart wide open
You will make space for the music
And that lets in the love
The more you hold
The more you have to give

BERNADETTE SOMERS

Here Comes the Sun *

Here Comes the Sun is a famous Beatles song written by George Harrison. The song emerged as George picked up a guitar and wandered through the garden belonging to his friend, Eric Clapton. He has described how the song just arrived as he enjoyed a beautiful day in the garden. And it arrived, just like the sun, with a simple and happy melody. That's how the sun makes me feel: happy.

I have always written poems, ever since I was a young girl. I always found it simple to make things rhyme. I could see words in my mind that just seemed to fit together. Just like sunshine and happiness fitting together.

I think I draw on this skill to write my songs and books. I have a clear memory of being in class in Grade 6 where I was asked to write a poem detailing what I loved about summer. It was a simple task. I just had to write about the sun and being outdoors, just like George Harrison did. I vividly remember the lines of my poem:

'Eating ice cream, nice and cool

Getting sunburnt by the pool.'

My teacher was impressed with my poem and asked me to read it out to the class. I remember the class's reaction when I said the word, 'sunburnt'.

---

* Written by George Harrison, 1969. Publisher: Wixen Music Publishing Inc. Quoted under Fair Use Act.

Everyone was bemused as to why I had not written sun tanned. Getting sunburnt was surely not something you loved about the summer. I remember considering for the first time that other people tanned in the sun. I thought everyone got burnt by the sun, like me. I had fair skin and blue eyes and my idea of a tan was the scattering of freckles.

Even so, I never feared the sun or getting burnt, the sun just made me happy.

It is only as I have got older and made several trips around the sun, that the collectives' feelings about the sun seemed to have changed. It is now seen as something we need to protect ourselves and cover up from.

Our skin must be free of any signs of the sun: freckles get covered with makeup or removed, sunspots are lasered away and tans come from a spray or a bottle. It's like we have to erase any signs that the sun has been on our skin. And it made me wonder why the sun has been demonised.

The sun is a 4.5 billion old star that has been the giver of energy, light and life to us all and without it, none of us would exist.

It brings us light, not harm. Plants grow towards it, not hide from it, yet we spray our plants with chemicals and then ingest them. The sun provides us with Vitamin D, yet we spray our skin with chemicals, which could perhaps block its absorption.

I think the world gets a lot of things wrong, and I think we are conditioned to live in fear of many things that should not be feared.

I think we need the sun. George Harrison wrote *Here Comes the Sun* as he was feeling overwhelmed with the business side of producing music. He wanted to retreat from the scheduling and stress of all of it. He wanted to retreat to the sun. He didn't want to hide from it. He wanted to replenish in it.

While most of us are already aware of sensible sun exposure, I want to instead shed some light on the good things the sun does for us. I am here to write about things and bring a different lens to what we think we know. I am here to honour the sun, and I am here to honour a song that does the same.

It is a simple, happy beat that makes you feel content and warm, just like being in the sun.

I now look at my skin now with a different view. It has been many times around the sun and tells a story with its markings and freckles. It has been years since my skin has been clear, as the song lyrics say, but that is nothing to be ashamed of or cover up. It is something to honour and accept.

The skin might be a little more delicate in some areas and need a bit more love and nourishment. But it doesn't need scolding for having witnessed the sun. The sun brought me warmth and comfort.

People often use the slang expression that the sun 'beats down'. It makes it sound like the sun is merciless. I like to think the sun has a different kind of beat. It's the beat to which we all grow towards the light. And we all need the light.

Elton John laments that it feels like losing everything when the sun goes down.[*] I don't want that feeling. I want to feel the sun, always. I need its light.

---

[*] *Don't Let the Sun Go Down on Me*, written by Bernie Taupin and Elton John, 1974. Publisher: Universal Music Publishing Group. Quoted under Fair Use Act.

Nothing Breaks Like a Heart *

Some mornings when I am in my kitchen, going about my business, I catch myself singing a song. I seem to be singing but unaware that I am doing it, and the song is coming through my subconscious mind. The lyrics of a song always have a profound message for me.

My work as an intuitive renders me uncertain of what the day will bring and what 'work' life has in store for me. You see, I am only one small part of the workings already in play, and life, I like to say, is one hundred steps ahead of me. I just have to play my part and fit into the beat of it all.

This particular morning, I heard myself singing, *Nothing Breaks Like a Heart*. You might assume that I had heard the song on the radio or on the television but that's not the case. This song came out of the blue, and I didn't realise how much the lyrics would end up having a greater meaning for me.

A regular client texted me requesting a guidance session. She was having issues with family relationships and differences of opinion, courtesy of the pandemic turning everything on its head. She was feeling 'heartbroken'. Things were cutting her just like a knife.

---

* Written by Clement Picard, Conor Syzmanski, Ilsey Juber, Mark Ronson, Maxime Picard, Miley Cyrus and Thomas Brenneck, 2019. Publisher: BMG Rights Management, Sony/ATV Music Publishing LLC, Universal Music Publishing Group. Quoted under Fair Use Act.

A close family member had cut her off and shunned her children because of her personal views about vaccination. She was being punished for not toeing the line even though she felt, in a myriad of ways, the line had been crossed. She was being treated as if she was a child who must follow her parents' lead and represent their stance and ideals, rather than follow her own knowingness as an adult. She felt she was letting down her parents by following her own heart.

It is apparent to me how much the pandemic that began in late 2019 affected hearts: not just in a medical or health related way, but on a much deeper level. I know many people were left questioning how the virus affected their heart. Others were left questioning how the vaccines affected the heart. For me, it felt the pandemic cut to the very cord of the heart, deep into the heart's intelligence.

Often, we focus on all the factors that affect the heart: diet, exercise, smoking and alcohol. We focus on the medical risk factors that compromise the heart. But I believe that we fail to recognise how other factors compromise the heart like pain, sadness, grief, isolation and division. Emotions are stored in the heart. And nothing breaks like the heart.

There is scientific evidence that the recipients of transplanted hearts have changes to their personalities and emotions after receiving a donor heart. It is postulated that the cells of the heart have a cellular memory of all that was recorded and stored in the heart. This, along with the heart, is passed on to the recipient.

So, I believe there is reason to explore the abilities of the heart, not only as the organ to help blood to flow, but as an organ contributing to the 'flow' of the person for whom it beats. The higher and ongoing incidence of heart-related conditions post-covid, made me consider the effects of isolation, lack of physical contact, separation, division, and the polarising differences of opinion on our hearts. The heartbreak of all of these factors caused hearts to break.

My client was facing exactly this. She was trying to navigate her life in a way forward that honoured her own heart, her own beat, her own perspective, despite her stance being at odds with her mother.

When we are intrinsically linked to the beat of our mother's heart through birth, it can cause great heart ache when mother wounds occur during our lives. Feeling unloved by our mothers can create a wound so deep, it can break hearts. Pain and sorrow are carried and stored somewhere. A heavy, burdened heart cannot beat in rhythm if under duress. Hearts must be open and free of wounds, in order not to break.

So, for anyone reading these words who has wounds that run as deep as their hearts, bring them to the light to heal. Gently open the heart to release the wounds All hearts need to beat freely and need blood to flow without impedance. Our lives need to flow without wounds impeding this flow.

I actually believe that every time our hearts expand, they 'break' open. It's an opening process. They break free of stored wounds. We all run deep, deeper than the surface vessels. We are the vessels, and we need to beat in time with each other and for each other.

Look after your precious heart. Keep the beat. It is your life force.

How will you play your hand?
With a club to fight in anger?
With a spade to dig and bury your pain?
Or with a diamond to reflect the light in order to see
That the heart always wins

BERNADETTE SOMERS

Tiny Dancer *

What do you hold close to your heart? What do you need to be close to the beat? What need to feel close, right there, warm against the chest? I always think we want to keep the things that matter most to us close, just like a mother holds her baby close to her chest. It's a physical thing, but it's also something deeper. I think we want to keep things close to our heart, close to the beat. I think that the beat means much more than we can fathom. It's the connection to everything and everyone. It draws us in to where we all want to be held.

It's fascinating to me to watch musicians try to 'hold' the beat, their faces holding a look of intensity balanced with concentration. Poised. Ready. Like a child ready to jump into a moving skipping rope and find the rhythm. Unless we sync to the rhythm of life, we may never quite enter into the moving rope. I feel like life needs motion and energy and we need the beat to instigate that motion and get things in flow. I guess that's how the heart is designed: the beat brings in the flow. So, it makes sense to me that we want to hold things close to that beat.

Tiny Dancer reminds me of a child trying to step in time to the beat of the music, trying to draw on something both innate and

---

*   Written by Bernie Taupin and Elton John, 1971. Publisher: Universal Music Publishing Group. Quoted under Fair Use Act.

instinctive in order to join in with the rhythm. It's that same look on the face. Poised. Ready.

Sung by Elton John, *Tiny Dancer* is such an iconic song, but I personally don't think it's because of the lyrics. I think it's more to do with the beat. When Bernie Taupin penned the words, he was trying to capture a feeling of California's spirit and the women from there.

For myself, the song captures a feeling, but its more to do with wanting to be held closer. We all want to be held closer and we all want things held close to our hearts. And when we hold each other closer, our hearts connect, not only in space, but in time—in time with the beat.

I think that we should never ever underestimate the power of holding people and things closer to our hearts. It's where we belong: close.

Tiny Dancer might be your reminder to hold all things close. It is my reminder, and the song evokes that beautiful feeling for me. It's just like holding a beat or playing an instrument. It soon becomes second nature.

I like to think that the flutters of love in my heart feel exactly like a tiny dancer, a tiny dancer making small light movements, creating a gentle feeling and presence that feels exquisite, almost like the flutters of an unborn baby's movement in the womb. Poised. Ready for birthing and to be held close to the mother's heart.

When a new baby is born, he or she is placed on the mother's chest. Right next to the beat: where all things long to be held.

The Twelfth of Never *

This is a song that is much older than me and it tells of a day and date that will never come to pass. It is the song that reminds me of my grandfather Bob because it was played at his funeral service. The song mentions bluebells, and bluebells are my grandfather's calling card.

My grandmother Ellen, Bob's wife, used to tell me a story. She said that when I was very little and didn't use my words to speak, I would be walking next to my grandfather Bob and want him to carry me. I would not speak but I would stand in front of him so that he would know to pick me up. We had this unspoken communication.

My papa Bob remains with me and still uses this unspoken communication with me. He sends bluebells. He relays very beautiful messages to me, for my mother. He still communicates, and when he wants to make his point clear he sends the bluebells. I think this is partly why my favourite colour is blue.

And the lyrics of my song, *Still With Me*, has bluebells in it to honour my grandfather Bob. I believe he is still with me. I will always feel a very strong need to honour those who have gone before me. And so, using a song to do that feels incredibly fitting. It keeps them

---

* Written by Jerry Livingston, Paul Francis Webster, 1958. Publisher: Spirit Music Group, Universal Music Publishing Group. Quoted under Fair Use Act.

with the beat.

My papa Bob was a very wise man with many of his own phrases and sayings that I often hear myself repeating. They have been relayed to me from my mother, his daughter, and I believe that Bob lives on in those words. I hope he lives on in these words too.

On one particular day he had some words of advice for my mother and in order to make his point clear, he sent her a bluebell. My mother was pottering outside in her courtyard garden, quietly tending to her garden, just like Bob would have done when he was alive. She had recently received some guidance from her father via me: the bridge. As she looked around her garden beds, she noticed one small bluebell growing in the most obscure place all on its own. She had never planted the bluebell, and she immediately thought of her father. This single bluebell flower was clear, and it helped to transcribe the message that Bob was imparting to his daughter.

There are many ways that our departed loved ones can get our attention and make their points clear. Their love is as endless as the date, which is the twelfth of never. They continue on in the signs, in the flowers, in their songs and in the beat.

Bluebells often grow in the place where Bob's ashes were scattered, right next to the ashes of his love, Ellen.

They remain together, until the twelfth of never.

Fly Like an Eagle [*]

I would like to fly like an eagle and let my spirit be carried. I would like to be free, like the feeling and like the song.

The eagle is a bird that is referenced in the lyrics of many songs and is even the name of a well-known and iconic band, The Eagles.

It is the bird that best represents the yearning for freedom. Sometimes when songwriters create lyrics, they want same kind of freedom so that their thoughts and ideals can be freely told in their song. Sometimes artists and musicians want that kind of freedom so that they can be fully self-expressed in their art.

In the 1970s the Steve Miller Band produced the song *Fly Like an Eagle*. The 70s was a time that reflected society's desire for cultural change and evolution. It was a decade known for rebellion against authority, personal liberation, and the pursuit for freedom. This song sings about the revolution. And a revolution involves wide-reaching change.

This line of the song about time slipping into the future was playing in my head as I awoke at 3:44 am. I have mentioned that I always see 44 as a number sequence. And I often receive songs and words 'between' 3 and 4 am. That hour of the night is known as a time when life whispers to those who are listening.

---

[*] Written by Steven Haworth Miller, 1996. Publisher: Sailor Music. Quoted under Fair Use Act.

It is magical and a little annoying at the same time, because I always feel the need to get up out of bed and write down what I hear so it isn't lost. Some sections of my book *Yolk* were written between 3 and 4 am.

This particular night was a restless night where sleep came in intervals and my mind was receiving 'in between'. I woke and looked at the clock in my bedroom to confirm the time of 11:59 am. I realised that the day was in its final moment. So, I decided to thank the day, in my thoughts. I'd had a good day, so I thanked the day for that. I honoured the day as it was departing.

In hindsight, I could have chosen to wait until 12:00 am and welcome the new day and focus on that. But it felt that the old day was 'slipping' and I focused on its final moment.

I thought about staying up late as a child on New Year's Eve, to welcome the new year and witness the old one slip away. I thought about how I never really focused on the slipping away, but more on the new year arriving. And I mused that many people are spending their lives waiting for the new to arrive. Looking to the new. Looking for the new. Not thanking the old. I considered the fleeting nanosecond that occurs 'between' the two before it all changes, and it made me think that life is fleeting and held and contained in that space between two worlds. It passes ever so quickly, in this fleeting part in between. We often spend it doing two things: looking back at what slipped away or looking at what is arriving in the future. We rarely stay in that fleeting middle space in between.

Much like the space between two days, our hearts never get to rest in the space between the beats. They work tirelessly for us. As every day slips away and we are resting, they are still working for us. I wonder whether the heart relies on the nanoseconds of rest found between the beats. I wonder if this space in between is where it finds its repose. I wonder if our lives aren't meant to be spent tirelessly working, like our hearts, without ever finding the repose.

FLY LIKE AN EAGLE

I wonder many things, many of which arrive between 3 and 4 am. I know life is whispering these important messages and song lyrics to me for a reason, if only just to write them here for you to contemplate. I know that if I can remain in the space between sleep and listening, I will always continue to hear. And I will always continue to share. This sharing is important to my heart, which works tirelessly for me. These musings and thoughts help to open my heart and that reduces its work. It also steadies the beat, and this gives my heart a welcome repose.

You rise with the sun
You birth with the moon
You sit with the stars
In flowers you bloom
You hold with the light
And swim with the sea
You move with the wind
And still with the breeze
You are all, you are one, in you, in me
We are one, born of one, part of one, we see
We move, we breathe, we are fire, we are sun
Of earth, of wind, of air, we become

BERNADETTE SOMERS

Money Money Money *

Sometimes the lyrics in a song aren't true. I don't believe it is 'always sunny' in a rich man's world. I think we all have to endure all seasons and all weather in life. Some would argue that money might make things a little easier to weather, but money doesn't leave with us when we depart. And what we leave behind can often cause many to argue.

You don't need money in the next dimension. That dimension is a rich man's world, a richness that I have tried to illustrate with the music and beat of this book. All our possessions stay behind; we might be able to bequeath them to someone else, but many spend their lives accumulating a wealth that is not of any value on the other side. What is of value is the legacy we leave, the person we were, the relationships we formed and the joy we created. I believe people remember our hearts, and so, it is fitting to be reminded of this in a book about the beat and a chapter about money.

The song by ABBA reflects a belief that many people hold: that we could do many more things in our lives if we had more money. When wanting to write this book and record the songs, I did think

---

* Written by Göran Bror Benny Andersson and Björn K. Ulvaeus, 1976. Publisher: BMG Rights Management, Exploration Group LLC, Sony/ATV Music Publishing LLC, Universal Music Publishing Group. Quoted under Fair Use Act.

about the money. I didn't want to compromise my family and the money we have to utilise for other things, but I wanted to leave a legacy. I wanted to leave my beat. I wanted my words and songs to stay after I have left. I'm assured that my beat will continue on.

It wasn't so much about the 'products' of myself, the book or the songs that I wanted to leave behind. It's more about the feelings they evoke. I hoped to stay present in the feelings and hopefully in the joy too. I visualised my grandchildren reading the words and feeling me close from wherever I was residing. I pictured the faces of those yet to arrive, listening to the songs and receiving the beat. I think this is what all departed singers and artists do. They live on in the beat.

I imagined all of the hearts opening as the music flooded in, and I understood that through the doorway of open hearts, I could still reach people. Not with my hands or no-longer-beating heart but with the beat of the music. This is what all who have passed can do: they can reach us through and with the music. We are connected through the beat.

I think we are remembered with the feelings that music provides. Maybe this, and our legacy, is enough.

When contemplating the mystery and magic of all of this I decided not to let money be my obstacle. If songs were coming to me in my dreams, if lyrics were being written in my mind, if guidance about the book was coming through, then I knew that the money could also come through. Money is energy; it moves through.

The global pandemic illustrated to us all the economic impact of stopping the flow of money. Shutting the world down affected the flow of all things energetic. Money is one of these things. It needs to flow between us all and the cycle of giving and receiving needs to be continued. Money doesn't need to be viewed as anything but a continual moving energy. It doesn't have to have attachments and negative connotations, or beliefs associated with it. It just needs to move through. It needs to keep moving through economically and it needs to be moved through emotionally.

However, many people are conditioned to view it as something negative, or not within their reach. Many people take on the money mindset of their parents. If money was scarce, they can take on that scarcity mindset and let it permeate into other aspects of their lives. Life can feel capped in its opportunities and resources. The heart can be closed to receiving.

If money was seen as the root of all evil, then those with money might be seen as entitled or spoilt. This can cause resentment, jealousy and unhappiness. The heart can be closed to giving.

I guess my point is, money affects the heart, it affects the beat. And just like blood needs to move through our hearts, money and its many attachments need to be released.

I decided not to allow money to be a determining factor in me expressing myself and my open heart throughout this book.

I was not going to let a lack or scarcity mindset affect the birthing of *Beat*. I chose to feel abundant. I chose to let my heart give and receive.

I have a habit of not wanting to proceed with things if I feel they will compromise another person. I factor in my family, the six of us, into all the decisions I make. It is like the six of us are one, and we must all mutually benefit from my choices. It's not a limiting or negative way to live, it's actually a beautiful way to live. It is considered. I consider things before I step forward. I feel I step with and for my family. We all step together.

It's like the lyrics of the song *(Everything I Do) I Do It for You* by Bryan Adams.* Everything I do, I do for the six of us. When writing

---

* Written by Bryan Adams, Michael Arnold Kamen and Robert John Lange, 1990. Publisher: Fintage House Publishing, Kobalt Music Publishing Ltd., Universal Music Publishing Group. Quoted under Fair Use Act.

Yolk, I wanted to be sure that the six of us were all comfortable with me being out of the spiritual closet. It's kind of like diving under water together as a unified six. I can't get too carried away with diving too deep if one of the other five needs to come back up for air. So, I step forward, but it's a considered step, just like writing this book.

There is nothing left to hide. I am here in all the words and songs; I am here in the beat. And I hope I get to stay here. I hope I live on in these words so I remain with my six, forever into eternity. Everything I do, I do for them.

I wrote in an earlier chapter about feeling that I was here on earth to find some sort of deeper meaning, lay some roots and leave some of myself behind. This is me trying to leave a part of myself behind. In the beat.

I hope that my six, the family unit that is us, fully understand that after reading this. I wrote for me. I sung for me. But I also wrote and sung for us all. The six of us, always united in the beat.

Perfect *

'Perfect' is a word I write a lot. It is also a word I sing a lot. My favourite song to sing in my cover band, is *Perfect* by Vanessa Amorosi. But there are multiple songs with the title *Perfect*, including the songs sung by Ed Sheeran, One Direction, Pink, Fairground Attraction and Selena Gomez. My business name is Perfect Balance Wellness, and I therefore use the word 'perfect' frequently. But I am anything but perfect.

I have had to make peace with the word 'perfect.' I have had to understand that my word and meaning 'perfect' now implies a personal perfect, just like people strive for a personal best or PB. I strive for a PP: personal perfect. It's actually a form of 'imperfectly perfect,' and I have made peace with that.

If it wasn't such a hassle, I would remove the word 'perfect' from my business name and vocabulary. But the easier option is to make peace with the word and find a new meaning for it.

When listening to the beat of all the songs named 'Perfect', there are many different meanings in the lyrics. Some songs depict the kind of perfect bliss found in romantic relationships. Other songs illustrate the unhealthy nature of perfectionism, that is, holding unrealistic high standards and unattainable benchmarks, as if things

---

* Written by David Franj and Vanessa Amorosi, 2008. Publisher: Universal Music Group. Quoted under Fair Use Act.

have to be absolutely perfect to be worth it.

Unhealthy perfectionism is becoming more engrained in our culture and is a contributing factor to the rising number of people diagnosed with anxiety, depression, eating disorders and obsessive-compulsive disorders. At lot of personal value is measured by educational and professional achievements and many people strive to prove their worth through unrealistic goal setting. Moreover, parents often pass their own achievement anxieties onto their children.

Perfectionism can be deemed a healthy attribute when it facilitates striving for attainable standards and goals. Sports psychology studies have shown that Olympic bronze medallists appear happier than the silver medallists. It is thought that the silver medallists compare themselves to the gold medallists and see their achievement as substandard. Yet, the bronze medallists compare their result to finishing in fourth place and not receiving a medal and are thus happy to receive the bronze. So much of what we deem as perfect is in the eye of the beholder.

The Japanese honour the imperfect in the practice of Kintsugi, a process of repairing broken pottery with powdered gold. The philosophy known as wabi-sabi embraces the flawed or imperfect and views the imperfections as part of an object's story and purpose.

If only society could learn to honour the imperfect and not strive to hide the damage and cracks because they understand that this is where the light gets in. Instead of indulging in a world where there is mass production and quick disposal, imagine if society could maintain optimism when things fall apart and see the beauty in the repair and the repurposing.

I believe we have a lot to learn about creating a perfect world, and we could start finding more purpose by reappropriating the word 'perfect'. We could find new purpose by framing the imperfect as perfect. We could aim for healthy perfectionism and accept the learnings and lessons in the faults and imperfections. We could strive for our own 'repurposed' personal best and honour the imperfect results.

We have a lot to learn from all the different songs about perfection and how we view our own sense of 'personal perfect'. It just might be time for all of us to sync to a new beat and find our own way to perfectionism.

Under Pressure [*]

I woke one night to the lyrics of *Under Pressure* playing in my head. I knew life had a message for me and I wasn't sure if I wanted to hear it. I had been feeling a bit 'under pressure' trying to work to the timelines I had set for myself. One of my default settings is to put pressure on myself to reach the standards I have set for myself, while completing tasks in an acceptable timeframe. This ends up being a battle of wills between my mind and body.

If I feel under pressure, my body manifests this as symptoms. If I am not feeling steady with the pace of life, I tend to trip over. If I am feeling there's an urgency to getting things done, my bladder likes to present with some urgency. If I am not feeling grounded, I tend to develop issues with my feet. These are just some examples of how my body communicates what occupies my mind.

It has taken me years to understand the signs and symptoms and see the messages in the symptoms. The whole area of mind-body connection fascinates me and has now become a big facet of my work. But if I am not getting the hint from my symptoms, life gifts me lyrics, and I woke to realise that I was indeed 'under pressure'.

---

[*] Written by Brian Harold May, David Bowie, Freddie Mercury, John Richard Deacon and Roger Meddows Taylor, 1981. Publisher: Sony/ATV Music Publishing LLC, Warner Chappell Music, Inc. Quoted under Fair Use Act.

UNDER PRESSURE

Under Pressure is a song performed by two of the greats: David Bowie and Freddy Mercury. If you listen to the lyrics, it feels as if it is a battle of wills. It reminds me of the polarity of life: fear and love. David Bowie sings the fear-based lyrics whilst Freddy Mercury sings about giving love a chance towards the end of the song. The result feels like a battle between the singers and the lyrics. It is reported to have also been a battle to birth this song due to the artists' differing opinions of how it should be produced. Like all good battles, there is always an outcome—and this was a favourable one. The song became a huge success. David Bowie and Freddy Mercury, both powerful artists in their own right, needed to work together in order to find harmony.

I see the correlations between our minds and bodies. Our minds and our bodies are powerful forces, but they also need to work in harmony. Often our minds put our bodies 'under pressure' by pushing through resistance and ignoring signs and symptoms. We set mental timelines and deadlines that our bodies can struggle to keep up with. Our bodies try to alert us to issues, with symptoms, but often we battle against them. We blame our bodies for their failings instead of heeding the messages in the symptoms.

Love challenges us to find a new way to care for ourselves, as the lyrics in this song convey. I think we need to relieve the pressure, pace of life, timelines and deadlines. I think we all need to sync to a new beat on the street that allows us to progress at a pace that suits our bodies. I think we need to reset our minds to take greater care of our bodies and treat them with the love and nourishment they need.

I was ignoring the symptoms, and so life gave me a song with a beat to bring me back to my heart. I needed to take the pressure off myself and listen to my body. I needed to stop pushing through and allow rest when I required it.

I guess it's a different beat to how we are all conditioned to live.

We have learnt to value productivity and being busy over rest and relaxation. We have learnt to tune into our minds and tune out from our bodies. However, in doing so, we aren't in tune with our hearts.

If we listen, our hearts will tell us if our practices and lifestyles are serving us or not. We just need to tune into the beat.

So, ask yourself if you feel you are under pressure, then ask yourself if you are tuning in or tuning out. You get to decide the outcome.

Stairway to Heaven [*]

I once had a dream that I was climbing a stairway to heaven. The dream felt so vivid and lucid. When I got to the top of the stairway, I was surprised to see that it was not that different to how things were at the bottom of the stairs. It had all the same things, all the things I love and treasure, but I felt continual bliss. This feeling was constant, like a never-ending weekend. I felt like there was nothing I had to do, I could just be.

They say that the most common day to suffer a heart attack is on a Monday, straight after the weekend. This idea made me ponder whether our hearts can sense that 'bottom of the stairway' feeling, back to Monday, longing again for the weekend—an absence of bliss. This made me wonder whether we spend our whole lives waiting for the weekend instead of finding the bliss in every day and every moment.

Do we enjoy the view, or do we spend all our time and energy climbing up the stairway to seek it? My grandfather Jim once came to me from the top of the stairway with a very important message. It was related to his son, my father, but the message in his words can be applied to all of us, and all of our lives.

He said that my dad was 'his father's son but equally his own

---

[*] Written by Jimmy Page and Robert Plant, 1971. Publisher: Warner Chappell Music, Inc. Quoted under Fair Use Act.

man'. He was dealt a similar hand of cards, but he, like all of us, held the trump card. I was waiting eagerly to hear what this magic trump card was. Would it be something that could help my father with his health issues? Was it some miracle tablet? Or something that could help him win this hand, win this battle, and defy the hand of cards he had been dealt? What was the trump card? Was it the joker, the king, the queen, the ace?

My grandfather said very clearly, 'It is the card of positivity.'

And I understood in that moment what he was teaching me. He was referring to the same message in the lyrics of 'Stairway to Heaven', to the woman 'who sees all that glitters as gold'. Every day is her weekend. I think that if the heart can sense it's a Monday and it feels like it's at the bottom of the stairs, then I wish to spend my life feeling like every day is the weekend too. I want to feel I am at the top of the stairway, enjoying the view.

According to my lucid dream, the scenery was much the same, but the feeling was one of bliss. I have mentioned that I see codes in words or specific double meanings, just like the lyrics of 'Stairway to Heaven' remind us that words can have two meanings.

The commonly used abbreviations of Saturday and Sunday are 'sat' and 'sun'. And if you take the abbreviations from the weekend and 'sat in the sun', it would glitter like gold. There would be nothing to do and it would feel like the weekend. You would just get to 'be' in your bliss, the kind where you feel like you're at the top of the stairway to heaven enjoying the view.

Led Zeppelin's Stairway to Heaven is a convoluted song with different meanings, different melodies and a lot of light and shade—a true resemblance of life. But I prefer to feel the light, sit in the sun and focus on the bliss. I prefer to play my trump card.

This is how I try to live my life.

This is my stairway, my heaven.

And this is where you'll find me: sitting in the sun, enjoying the view. This is my bliss.

Heal Me *

Lady Gaga sings a beautiful song called *Heal Me* in the soundtrack of the 2018 film *A Star Is Born*.†

I know a beautiful lady who was born just after the first iteration of *A Star is Born* was released. Her father, Bill, named her after a star. Bill was a captain who navigated ships and relied on the stars for direction. He used nautical charts and compasses but also relied on his instincts and intuition. He watched the stars move from east to west, watched them rise and fall, and found his own way to navigate.

Bill's daughter grew up to become a healer, and like her father, she also learnt to navigate by relying on instinct and intuition. She would help navigate her own son through a health issue. Her son was named Billy after her father.

I have had songs arrive for myself with healing in the lyrics, but I have never had songs arrive through me for someone else. Until I connected with Bill. Bill knew how to navigate in life and also his afterlife. I wonder if he still relied on the stars. He was able to help

---

*   Written by Lady Gaga, Mark Nilan Jr., Nick Monson, DJ White Shadow, Julia Michaels and Justin Tranter, 2018. Publisher: Sony/ATV Songs LLC / House of Gaga Publishing LLC (BMI). Quoted under Fair Use Act.

†   Screenplay by Eric Roth, Bradley Cooper and Will Fetters, based on 1954 screenplay by Moss Hart. Directed by Bradley Cooper. Distributed by Warner Bros. Pictures

direct me how to best deliver his message to his girl. He used music, relying on the beat.

I was about to pass on his channelled message to his daughter in an intuitive reading when he instructed me to record her a song. This was the first and only time this has happened to me. I sat at my piano and pressed record on my phone and the song called *Why* came through.

The song was for his daughter and remains hers, but I will share the lyrics.

You wonder why
You're wondering why
You ask yourself why
You need to know why

It's for you
It's to help you
It's to show you the way
Back home to me

I'll show you why girl
I'll show you why girl
I'll show you why
It's the way home for you
And for him too

I'll show you why girl
I'll show you why girl
I'll show you why

Follow the stars
Follow your star
Follow the stars
Follow your star

Follow the stars my girl
I'm leading you home
Follow the stars
Follow your star

BERNADETTE SOMERS

Bill had a song for his daughter, called *Why*. He had the same name as his grandson, Billy, the only difference being the letter 'Y'.

His message for his girl was to encourage her to help her son with his health issue: she could heal him. And if she understood that she could heal him, she would understand 'why' he was her son and she was his mum. With the guidance, she could see that it all made sense, she had her 'why'.

This woman had many skills that helped her to heal others, but she hadn't realised that she could also heal her son. Her father helped to direct her, just like he directed the ships according to the stars. He was still helping his daughter and helping her to navigate.

As the lyrics in the *A Star Is Born* song describe, the daughter was to treat her son like a patient. Other lyrics in *Heal Me* have the same resonance as Bill's message. The first movie this daughter ever attended was *A Star Is Born*. She was only a few weeks old. Her father Bill held her during the movie and paced the side aisles of the cinema to settle her to sleep. He kept her close to the beat of his heart and gave her peace.

Through his song, I believe he still keeps her close to the beat, bringing her peace. She instils this peace into her beautiful son Billy, his grandfather's namesake. He too is guided by the stars and his beautiful mum. This gives meaning to the 'why'.

We often search for the answers as to 'why' something is happening to us or when it might be happening for us, here might be reasons why. Trusting in the stars to help direct us might help us all to find our way home.

Even Flow *

I think we would all love our lives to be in an even flow. We would like there to be more growth without the lessons. More flow without the ebb. More gains without the losses.

I love the line from Pearl Jam's song *Even Flow* that reminds us that butterflies can fly in like thoughts.

I am known for my love of butterflies. They are my sign from departed loved ones and the logo for my business. Artwork of butterflies are scattered throughout my home, and there is even a butterfly on the spine of my first book *Yolk*.

Eddie Vedder, the vocalist and writer of *Even Flow*, was referencing a homeless man he had encountered when he wrote the lyrics of his song. The lyrics are a bit darker than the beautiful line about the butterflies, but I still see the similarities.

Once the butterfly leaves the cocoon, it is essentially homeless. It can't go back. And while the cocoon is safe and warm, it's not a place where we can stay forever. At some point we all have to leave the cocoon. I believe this is the hardest part of the journey.

Butterflies are amazing creatures. They use their antennae to balance, navigate and sense as they fly. They rely on sensations and feelings through these antennae. I think we are the same. Thoughts,

---

* Written by Eddie Vedder and Stone Gossard, 1991. Publisher: Universal Music Publishing Group. Quoted under Fair Use Act.

hunches, feelings, nudges and intuition can arrive like butterflies: subtle, quiet, flying in gently. We can sense them just like the butterfly uses its antennae or we can do exactly as the lyrics in the song describe: chase them away.

I honestly believe we are all gifted a life in order to transform it. I think we are meant to be learning, growing and feeling while immersed in the cocoon only to then emerge in full flight. I am not sure if this flight occurs in this lifetime, at the final ending or in the next lifetime. Maybe it's a little of all three.

However, I know that the butterfly doesn't live or last long after emerging from the cocoon. Once it has emerged from the protective shell, the average lifespan is only two weeks. It feels as if the whole point of the transformation was in fact the metamorphosis. The internal work. It's almost as if all the integral work is already done by the time the butterfly takes flight.

I wonder if the most important parts of our lives are not the parts when all is in 'even flow', but maybe the path that works toward this. Maybe the most important parts of the journey are the parts that require us to dig deep, bunker in and find our true selves in the process. Maybe this is what leads to the metamorphosis. Sometimes those hard times can feel like the darkness of a cocoon. Sometimes the real freedom is in breaking free.

I believe that life can be in more 'even flow' when we learn to work with our 'antennae' just like the butterflies do. I think we can practice leaning into life if we're attuned to our senses, feelings and intuition.

I think thoughts arrive like butterflies and we have a choice; we can focus on them or let them fly on through. We can choose to focus on the thoughts that don't lead to our suffering. And we can choose to let negative thoughts fly right through.

We can transform our minds and lives to allow more even flow. I believe all of this inner work is done in our own cocoon phase, our metamorphosis stage.

I think *Even Flow* might be a song about being homeless, but I choose to let the lyrics remind me of finding another way back home. By focusing on the transformation, the inner work, the parts of the journey that require more from me, I find myself in the process. I find my way back home.

I will always love butterflies because of what they represent to me. Once they transform and take flight, they don't return home. They don't need to, they have transformed. They fly. They are free. This is how I wish to be.

This is even flow. This is a beat to which I will always try to sync.

Fix You [*]

When you are underwater, you can't really hear the beat: it's muffled, unclear, murky and confused. The sound waves are lost in the physical waves. I think if you are going under, the lights might still be able to guide you home and bring you to the surface.

I would like to believe that. I would like to believe in the words of the song *Fix You*, that lights really could 'guide you home'.

I think of a coin sitting on the bottom of the ocean floor. If it catches the light, no matter how far down it is, it can still shine. It can still reflect the light. It can still be seen and saved.

It is no coincidence that people who are struggling to cope feel like they are sinking. This can be both the people who are going under and the caregivers who finally understand that they cannot 'fix' them.

Going underwater is a place to disconnect from sound. It is the depths we can sink to when we can't connect to the beat. *Underwater* is also the name of my song, and it's vulnerable and personal to share. It was written at a challenging time in my life and the life of my son. I believe it might help someone out there who has felt like my son and me. And my son cares deeply about helping others who

---

[*] Written by Christopher Anthony John Martin, Guy Rupert Berryman, Jonathan Mark Buckland and William Champion, 2005. Publisher: Universal Music Publishing Group. Quoted under Fair Use Act.

have felt like him. This is his 'share' as much as mine, and I have his blessing. He is in the beat as much as I am. This difficult time in my son's life has opened his heart to a beat that connects him to all who feel like he did.

Giving birth to a child is one of life's perfect miracles. Watching that child struggle with depression is like sinking underwater. My firstborn son was 17 years old when he was diagnosed with depression. This caused ripple effects in our whole family. To watch someone battle to stay afloat is crushing to watch. But to feel you are going under with them, is worse.

You cannot be a life support or buoy for someone if you sink with them. How do you choose who to save?

I told you in my first chapter that 'when I find myself in times of trouble, Mother Mary comes to me'.* She comes, and so do words, sounds, songs and lyrics. They help me process the heaviness of what I am feeling. Some people might find themselves venting in word form by writing or journaling. Some people might need to run to burn off steam. Some people might need to numb the feelings with alcohol, food or medication.

As for me, I turn to the beat. I go to my piano, and she witnesses it all. I call her 'she' because she feels like Mother Mary. She listens. She welcomes and accepts it all.

On the day I felt like I was sinking, she let me play *Underwater*.

---

* From *Let It Be*. Written by John Lennon and Paul McCartney, 1970. Publisher: Sony/ATV Music Publishing LLC Paul McCartney and John Lennon © Paul McCartney / Sony Music Publishing. Quoted under Fair Use Act.

UNDERWATER

Don't bring me down your road
I need my way
Can't go this time with you
Don't drag me underwater
I'm only holding on
Don't drag me down with you
Please listen

I am only holding on
By a gentle thread
I am holding on to
My line of faith to get me through this

Don't drag me
Drag me down and take me under
I need to breathe.
Please don't drag me underwater
I can only breathe a little
Please don't drag me under with you
I need to breathe
Look I know you're struggling
But I must self-preserve this time
I care for you so deeply
But I must breathe

Please don't drag me underwater
Please don't drag me underwater
Please don't drag me down
Don't drag me under, drag me under
I'm only just holding on

Can you hold on too
Can you hold on too
Can you hold on too

Please don't drag me underwater
I need to breathe
Don't drag me under

BERNADETTE SOMERS

When my son was having one of his worst days and was unable to move from his bed or find any joy in any moment, I went and laid with him. I laid my head on his chest and listened to his heartbeat. I told him that he was underground in a hole and could only see muddy walls, but the horizon was at ground level.

I told him that if he could hold on and trust his dad and me, we could both lift him to ground level. If he could hold on, we could lift. And from ground level, he could at least look ahead to see the horizon, see a future. I told him that I was at ground level with his dad and we could see what he couldn't from the hole underground. We could see his future, and it looked bright. He just couldn't see it below ground level.

I imagine being underground and underwater are similar places to be: at some point we all need to resurface. We all need to come back up for air.

I am not sure, but I think my words held light, perhaps they held air too, because I believe my son breathed them in. I don't think I 'fixed' him, but I certainly tried to.

I would have done anything, but I had to be afloat in order to be a life raft. I would like to believe that I gave him a vantage point of the view I held for him, the view I held in my heart. That view had so much light and the light might have helped to guide him home. I like to believe it did.

My son's experience gave him the greatest gift; he can connect to the beat of the hearts of all those who suffered like he did. And so, I wanted to share my deeply personal and raw song with you in the hope that it might help. Maybe you are walking similar steps to me or steps similar to my son. Maybe you are sinking underwater or feeling like you're underground.

Please stay at ground level.

Please see the view ahead. It looks beautiful.

And as I did for my son, I will hold that view for you, in my heart, right next to the beat.

DOWNLOAD
'UNDERWATER'
ON SPOTIFY

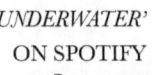

FIX YOU

Oh, I see you
I see you there
Hoping for some help
In your quiet despair
Praying for a change
Looking for a way
To ease the pain
And bring a new day
Waiting in the wings
Looking for a time
To sit in the space
Where it all feels fine
Oh, I see you
Hold on if you can
I'm sending you love
As much as I can

BERNADETTE SOMERS

Brave *

I resonate with the lyrics of the song entitled *Brave* by Sara Bareilles. The lyrics remind me to speak up, but more importantly, to always be brave.

I believe that we are in fact born brave and that bravery is our birthright. I like to think that making our way from the safety of our mother's womb at birth requires bravery.

The delivery itself is called labour, and I think this requires bravery from both the mother and the child. I like to imagine that bravery travels through the bloodstream, from the mother's heart to the unborn child. I hope that this helps the unborn child prepare for the life that is about to begin.

Perhaps the child is therefore equipped to face life 'head on' just as it is delivered headfirst into the world.

At this moment of my own birth, I was gifted the name Bernadette.

And my name means brave as a bear.

I never liked the name Bernadette when I was growing up. I much preferred my second name, Therese. The name Therese refers to a harvester: someone who collects resources for future use. I resonate with this, collecting stories and songs from my life and

---

* Written by Jack Antonoff and Sara Bareilles, 2013. Publisher: Sony/ATV Music Publishing LLC. Quoted under Fair Use Act.

reaping something from what I have sewn.

I never related to the name Bernadette.

I never considered myself to be brave, as my name denotes.

When my mother gave birth to me, she was unsure whether to name me Bernadette Therese or Therese Bernadette.

She asked a sister at the hospital, and she recommended that I was named Bernadette after Saint Bernadette. Mother Mary appeared to the young Bernadette Soubirous in Lourdes, France. Both Bernadette and Therese are names with French origins, and I do feel connected to both names. I also feel a connection to the story of Bernadette; she spoke up about something that was 'hard to explain and understand'.

I know I have mentioned that I love numbers and the numbers 4 and 44 specifically. Saint Bernadette was born in 1844. Her feast day is the 16th of April, the fourth month. I know I have said that I see words as codes and meanings in words. I see that Bernadette Soubirous's name as the same initials as I do in mine: Bernadette Somers.

As I have grown older and moved away from religion and towards spirituality, I have a newfound appreciation for my first name. I love the story of Saint Bernadette and how she spoke the truth of what she saw and heard. I also love her quote, 'My job is to inform, not convince'. I feel the same as her. The stories in this book are to inform, not convince you of anything. They are my truth, but you have your own. Even so, it feels liberating to express my truth.

I think of Saint Bernadette when I write about the things that are 'hard to explain and understand'. I think about how hard it must have been for her to explain what she saw and what she heard. I often feel the same.

I realise now that I do have to be brave—as 'brave as a bear'. I think I might get that bravery from my name, and from her.

But I think that the most magical and beautiful thing I notice about my name is that I see the word 'beat' in it.

BErnAdeTte

The beat is in my name. It is part of who I am. As a writer and a singer, it seems so incredibly fitting that I was named Bernadette.

I don't think the sister in the hospital would have ever imagined that the baby being named Bernadette would grow into a woman who would see so much meaning in the name she recommended. I am proud to put my name next to the beat. I am happy that I have written about things that required me to be brave.

I know there are many songs dedicated to girl's names; Angie, Billy Jean, Rhiannon, Jolene, Mandy, Cecilia, Sweet Caroline, Eleanor Rigby and Valerie, to name a few.

There is no song entitled 'Bernadette', and there may not be a song with your name. But you are brave, and the song *Brave* could be yours too.

I believe you can find the bravery to do things that are challenging. You can find it in you. It is as inherent in you as the bravery you were born with. It is part of you, just like the beat.

I am a woman who shares her songs that arrive from somewhere 'hard to explain and understand'. I am someone who writes about the beat, a word that lies within me and my name.

I am brave. We all are. I think our hearts hold our bravery, right next to the beat.

BRAVE

Place your hands on your heart
Feel the beat
Stay right there, for as long as you need
The beat is yours
Breathe in the feeling
Breathe in the air
Breathe in the light
Open your heart to the beat and let it expand
Feel it expand so much that you become light
Feel it lift you
Feel it take you home

BERNADETTE SOMERS

Heart of Stone [*]

Heart of Stone is arguably one of the Rolling Stones' most famous songs. I used to believe that stones were hard and heavy and certainly not the right word to describe a beautiful heart. I now think differently and it's all due to my nan. She helped me to see stones in a completely different way, and, unbelievably, she is and always remains only a stone's throw away from me.

I have written about my grandfather Robert, my nan's husband, and his bluebells. Robert used to collect stones: small, white, smooth stones to fill the drain lining the grass in his perfectly manicured backyard. Robert was always out pottering in his garden, much the same as he pottered through his life. The path lined with stones led down to his small humble studio where he repaired shoes. Robert was a shoemaker but could have been a gardener. He made the shoes so that we all could walk and be grounded and steady like he was. This is kind of how I remember him, slowly walking through his garden at the very same pace he walked through his own life.

I know a beautiful lady who works with stones. Not the type my grandfather collected, but more precious stones that are paired with gold and worn as jewellery. She had a baby too precious for this

---

[*] Written by Keith Richards and Mick Jagger, 1965. Publisher: Abkco Music Inc., BMG Rights Management, Unison Rights S.L.. Quoted under Fair Use Act.

world, just like a precious stone. He was golden and named Robert, just like my grandfather.

One morning, when meditating, my nan came through to convey a very important message. I was beginning to doubt the progress of my book and she had some wise words to reassure me. She had a beautiful message about stones.

She firstly said that she was safely delivering my daughter home on this day. She was due to return from her overseas travel. Nan said that my daughter was coming home safely and so was her ring, all stones intact. You may remember the chapter *I Got You Babe* and the story of my nan's precious ring. Nan then reminded me of Robert's path lined with stones. She showed me an image from my childhood when all the grandchildren would search for stones for Papa. Nan told me she was sending me stones.

I was a little puzzled until she explained that Papa's path was filled slowly and steadily, one by one, by stones. She said she was sending me signs, help, support and love, like little stones, and that one by one, my path would be clear and full. I cannot fully articulate how profound, wise and utterly beautiful Nan's message was, and how it completely transformed how I was feeling. I decided to trust her and the wisdom in her words.

I went outside to my garden where my nan's camelia plant was in bloom. I picked a camelia to put in a vase on my bedside table to remind me of her comforting words. I noticed that I had in fact picked two camelias instead of one and thought it was a perfect pairing of flowers, just as my nan and I were a perfect pairing.

I was in the process of putting together a women's circle and went to work on my website to add in the details. I needed some technical support and wished my daughter was home to assist me. I reminded myself to be grateful that Nan was bringing her home safely on this day. I thought I would finish the website work later in the week when she could help me but quickly put in a photo of me to represent the women's circle page on the website.

I decided to go to the florist shop near my home and buy myself some flowers. I walked past the jewellery store where the lovely lady works with precious stones. I remembered her Robert. I felt that my nan was urging me to go in to the store and talk to this lady about my book. I went in and chatted to her so that I could assure her that my book was also her Robert's book, his little beat lived on in the words. He was remembered, along with Robert, my grandfather, in the stories.

I realised why my nan was sending me stones. She was showing me how many small stones come together to line a path. She was illustrating that my book held not only my own stories, my own beat, but held the stories of others as well. I understood that my book was honouring many lives, not just my own. And we were all like stones, lining one path together.

I understood that life brings all of us stones to line our path. Just as The Rolling Stones sing about the girl who will never break, I realised that I too will never break. I will keep forging on, step by step, stone by stone, until the end.

I looked at my website a few days later to complete the unfinished work. I looked at the photo of myself—the woman who will never break. When I studied the photo that I had chosen to fill the spot for the women's circle, I realised that it was a photo that my husband took of me at the Stones winery in the Yarra Valley.

And then I noticed what I was holding in my hands.

Two white camelias, exactly like the two camelias from my nan's plant that were on my bedside table.

I cannot even begin to describe the wonder and awe of this moment.

My nan's presence in my life is my perfect pairing.

Her guidance helps me to navigate my life, like stones lining my path.

HEART OF STONE

I now love this perfect pairing of the words 'heart and stone' in the Rolling Stones song title.
A pairing like my nan and me.
A pairing like writing and singing.
A pairing like Beat and my own heart.

Unchained Melody [*]

I think that God did speed love to me on my wedding day and it came with this song. The song *Unchained Melody* reminds me of my wedding ceremony; not the beginning of the wedding, or walking down the aisle, but the ending, the walking out.

This was our exit song.

My husband chose this song for our exit and I think he would be more than likely to choose it again one day for his own exit song. It is just his song, and now, through our union, our marriage, our 'walking out' together, it has become our song. As such, it feels right to have this *Unchained Melody* as the exit song and final chapter of *Beat*. It makes for the perfect exit as I walk my book out into the world, unchained.

I love the word 'unchained'. It describes how I feel when I sing and write. To combine both my loves—writing and singing—in this book feels complete, just like this last chapter. It feels like a holy union.

Unchained Melody was top of the charts in the year I was born and made its resurgence in the 90s when I was married. It is very symbolic to me that it was the song of a movie that depicted life after death, something that resonates with me so deeply.

---

[*] Written by Alex North and Hyman Zaret, 1965. Publisher: Unchained Melody Pub LLC. Quoted under Fair Use Act.

UNCHAINED MELODY

The song was sung by one of the two men called The Righteous Brothers, who were not actually brothers after all. Rumour has it that the two singers tossed a coin to determine who would sing the song for the recording: Medley or Hatfield.

Hatfield won the toss. But in true, full circle, Medley sang the song at Hatfield's funeral. It became his 'exit song.'

It therefore feels full circle that I finish my book with this exit song. It feels, once again, that I am complete, that the holy union of word and song feels like a marriage: two parts making a whole.

The union of two singers brought this song to life so that it was unchained. And although the word unchained is only in its title and not in the lyrics, it perfectly describes how I feel at this exit point.

I feel as if I am finishing *Beat* but that I have also brought a beat back to life. I feel as if I have united two great loves of my life.

It feels complete; just like knowing one has lived a full life and it is time to exit.

I wonder if you have ever contemplated what would be your own exit song? The beat of a song that lives on in your memory after your heart has stopped beating. It's your 'walking out' song, like my song at my wedding, walking out to something new.

I believe that we don't finish with that finishing beat. I think we exit into something new and unchained. Many of the songs and stories in this book have illustrated my own unwavering faith in this. However, your faith is for you, as is your own beat. But I believe in the oneness of all, and that includes the beat.

I would like to believe that when our own hearts stop the beat, we join in the universal, endless beat of the collective.

So, this exit song is a beat to which the memories can connect and have more meaning. It becomes another beat that honours life, just like the heartbeat.

I hope that this chapter might encourage you to think of your own exit song, a beat that continues with you, a send-off to

BEAT

something new.
    My truth is that I need music in my life, not just at my exit.
    I need to write lyrics.
    I need to sing.
    I need words and music to express my love.
    God speeds that love to me, and it reaches my heart.
    I just had to be unchained to bring it through.
    I am an unchained melody.
    May the melody continue to play to the beat, long after my exit.

For I am all things
And all things are me
I am the sea, the stars, the moon,
And they look back at me
I am a force of nature
And nature is a force in me
I am one with the earth
And she smiles back at me
I encompass all
And all encompasses me
I need nothing to feel whole
As wholeness is me

BERNADETTE SOMERS

A Final Word

The world and the universe are filled with light.
Light and love.
The two go hand in hand, like waves and water.
Without one, there cannot be the other.
Light pours into the universe every moment, in waves.
Waves of light.
The quantum field teaches us that all things are made of waves, vibrating like strings on a violin, vibrating at different frequencies.
Our hearts emit waves, waves of love and waves of sound through the beat. Just as a collection of metronomes will synchronise to the same beat, so can our hearts if we keep them open.
If we keep our hearts open, we receive light. Waves of light merge with waves of sound. And synchronise. We are all meant to synchronise.
Many waves in water make up the container which is the ocean. Together, we are the container, comprised of all our waves of light and sound.
We can change our hearts by holding more light.
We can change our hearts by holding more love.
We can change the beat.
We can create waves.
May the beat of the music lift us to soaring heights, where the waves carry us to more light.

A FINAL WORD

May the light merge with the light.
And may you be free.
Connected always and in all ways to the beat.

I hope I have done the beat justice.

I hope I have connected you back to the music
and to your own heart.

I hope I have taken you within, to where the love resides,
right next to the beat.

I hope I have taken you within, to where the beat resides,
right next to the love.

I hope I have taken you within, to where the love resides,
right next to the light.

I hope your heart is full of love and light,
which continues on in the beat.

BERNADETTE SOMERS

Acknowledgements

Thank you to my friend Chloe Planinsek, the talented artist whose beautiful artwork graces the cover of *Beat*.

Thank you to the gifted Adrian Hannan at The SongStore for collaborating with me to record the soundtrack of *Beat*.

Thank you to the skillful Monique Christensen of Mono Unlimited for publishing *Beat*.

And finally, thank you to my beautiful family of six.

I could not write this book or sing the songs without the unwavering love and support from my husband, Mark, and my children, Joshua, Benjamin, Annelise and Jake.

This *Beat* is for us.

I love you all dearly.

About the Author

Bernadette Somers is an intuitive mentor, medium, physiotherapist, singer/songwriter and holistic healer.

For decades, Bernadette has been running her own business, Perfect Balance Wellness, where she offers intuitive guidance, and sound and energy healing to assist her clients in re-balancing mind, body and soul.

Bernadette's first book *Yolk* depicts connection in this life and beyond, containing a roadmap for tapping into what lies beneath the 'shell'. While *Beat* offers stories of love and the afterlife, illustrating how the essence of our departed loved ones continues to guide us.

www.ingramcontent.com/pod-product-compliance
Lightning Source LLC
Chambersburg PA
CBHW070253010526
44107CB00056B/2451